International Economics and Institutions

Editor
Hans-Jürgen Vosgerau

International Economics and Institutions

Axel F. A. Adam-Müller
Internationale Unternehmensaktivität, Wechselkursrisiko und Hedging mit Finanzinstrumenten
X, 191 Seiten. 1995

Angelika Eymann
Consumers' Spatial Choice Behavior
XII, 192 Seiten. 1995

Klaus Wälde

Convergence, Divergence and Changing Trade Patterns

Theoretical Inquiries into the Role of Preferences, Factor Accumulation, Technological Change and Government Intervention

Springer-Verlag Berlin Heidelberg GmbH

Klaus Wälde
University of Amsterdam
Department of Macroeconomics
Roetersstraat 11
NL-1018 WB Amsterdam, The Netherlands

Die Deutsche Bibliothek - CIP-Einheitsaufnahme
Wälde, Klaus:
Convergence, divergence and changing trade patterns: theoretical inquiries into the role of preferences, factor accumulation, technological change and government intervention / Klaus Wälde. - Heidelberg: Physica-Verl., 1995
(International economics and institutions)
Zugl.: Kiel, Univ., Diss.

ISBN 978-3-7908-0878-0 ISBN 978-3-642-50034-3 (eBook)
DOI 10.1007/978-3-642-50034-3

Originally published by Physica-Verlag Heidelberg in 1995.

42/2202-543210 - Printed on acid-free paper

Meiner Ma', meinem Pa',

und m. TT. TT.

Foreword and acknowledgement

First of all, I would like to thank my supervisor, Professor Dr. Horst Herberg for his comments and suggestions he made at various stages of my thesis. Pointing out weak points helped to improve the quality of my investigations considerably. In addition, I would like to thank him for giving me access to a very good working infrastructure at the Institut für Theoretische Volkswirtschaftslehre.

Various parts of this thesis have been presented at conferences and seminars. I would like to express my thanks to Michael Rauscher and Ernst Mohr for initiating research seminars at the University of Kiel and the Kiel Institute of World Economics, respectively. Nearly my entire dissertation was presented at these very stimulating and instructive seminars in a very cooperative and warm atmosphere and comments were very useful, especially by the initiators. My thanks also include seminar participants for comments, remarks and suggestions. Chapter 4 benefited a lot from discussions with Wolfgang Keller. Having encountered him during his stay at the Kiel Institute of World Economics was very important. I thank him for discussions and encouragement and for having shown me what economics can be. I wish him all the best for his future. Thanks also to Ingo Thomas for discussions and having checked some calculations. Other chapters were presented at the annual meetings of the Econometric Society, the Verein für Socialpolitik and the Royal Economic Society as well as at a seminar at the Tinbergen Institute, Amsterdam, The Netherlands. Useful comments were provided by participants, especially by Paul Tang. First comments on very preliminary versions of some chapters were provided by Richard Frensch and Jürgen Meckl, which were very encouraging.

So many others contributed, even without knowing it, that it is difficult to mention them all; some, however, should not be forgotten: Frank Stehling for his readiness to listen to questions of any kind, Uwe Rentmeister, Ludwig von Auer, Antje Höning, Matthias Salge, Günter Coenen, Hannes Bröcker, Jens Wabbler; Professor Fieger for his excellent lectures in mathematics at the University of Karlsruhe, Albrecht Mengel, the staff of the RZ Kiel, who were always extremely friendly and cooperative, all those providing the framework for doing research, especially Mrs. Müller of the library of the Kiel Institute of World Economics and finally those who wrote those wonderful textbooks without which I would never have advanced so far: Gandolfo (1986) on trade, Chiang (1974) on basic mathematics, Blanchard and Fischer (1989) on Macro and dynamics and Lorenz (1989) on non-linear dynamics. Of course, as always, all shortcomings, errors, omissions and other flaws are solely my own guilt and responsibility.

Thinking about the more important, non-professional, environment, I thank my parents, and my family in general, for their unconditional support in all respects during all of my studies. I dedicate this dissertation to them. Being at least of equal importance, I won't forget my friends, especially those, who could (and sometimes had to) enjoy all my moods during the last years; I am thinking, among others, of Maike Krause and my dear friend Jörg Steinbach.

Finally, I would like to express my gratitude to the Filterwerke Mann + Hummel GmbH for having covered some travel costs and, above all, to the state of Schleswig Holstein (and thereby, implicitly, to taxpayers) for having financed my thesis through a two-year scholarship. I do appreciate this scholarship a lot and hope to have fulfilled my duty by having done my best.

Contents

Chapter 1: Introduction

1. Introduction and overview

Until still few years ago, economic growth theory (going back to Solow, 1956; for an introduction cf. Burmeister and Dobell, 1970) predicted convergence of both growth rates and level of per capita income of economies which share identical preferences, technologies and same population growth rates, independently of initial conditions. Countries with a low capital stock grow faster than those with a higher capital stock, until, in the long-run, they all converge to a common constant growth rate. This prediction is due to the way how growth is "explained" in models of this kind. Growth of output per capita resulted, in the simplest model, from an exogenous growth of labour productivity (see e.g. Sala-i-Martin, 1990; Grossman and Helpman, 1991a, ch. 2). Since this increase of productivity is exogenously given, the model itself does not give any explanation of its source. The prediction of convergence of growth rates, itself, is very doubtful and observations show, that on an international level either convergence is not given at all, or that it takes a very long time.

The literature of the "new" theory of growth provides a rich variety of models whose theoretical implications range from divergence to convergence and thus offers much better working tools in order to analyze real world observations. These models (starting with Romer, 1986 and Lucas, 1988) explain growth of GNP or per capita income from within the model by including external effects such as a public stock of knowledge capital (e.g. Romer, 1990; Grossman and Helpman, 1991a) or learning-by-doing mechanisms (e.g. Romer, 1986) and do not require an exogenous mechanism of growth. Hence, the term *endogenous* growth theory. Put differently, endogenous growth theory models do explain *positive* long-run growth rates without having to base on exogenous effects, whereas models of the Solow type do not.

The following chapters are a theoretical inquiry into the reasons for convergence, divergence and, in a trade theoretic perspective, for a reversal of trade patterns (TPR), which has been observed after World War II for e.g. Japan (Balassa and

Noland, 1989; Grossman, 1990) or the Four Tigers (a good overview of empirical aspects can be found in the World Bank (1993) report "The East Asian Miracle"). TPR are often associated with an increase of the economic well-being of a country: Japan which formerly exported labour intensive goods became gradually an exporter of high-tech goods[1] and at the same time succeeded in increasing income per capita. Due to the close relationship, attention has also been paid to those phenomena.

The very first idea has been to interpret trade pattern reversals as a result of different time preference rates. Why should a country, whose population is more patient than another country's is, not succeed in a higher growth rate and therefore experience a shift in its production structure? Possible implications were investigated in a two-country Heckscher-Ohlin model with long-run positive growth rates due to technological external effects, taken from Grossman and Helpman (1991a, ch. 7). It turned out that the basic result can be highlighted in a more direct way in a simplified version (neglecting growth effects) which is given in chapter 2, entitled "On an additional condition for factor-price equalization in intertemporal Heckscher-Ohlin models". The result does not concern TPR but is related to factor-price equalization (FPE). We find that in a world with inter- and intra-industrial trade, FPE does not result from free trade in intertemporal Heckscher-Ohlin models, unless individual discount rates are equal. When this condition is violated and both countries lie within the cone of diversification, they produce both goods though factor prices are not equalized.

Chapter 3 "Unequal factor prices and incomplete specialization in a Heckscher-Ohlin model of endogenous growth", then presents the original Grossman and Helpman model, mentioned above, and strengthens the result of chapter 2 standing in contrast to the pure theory of international trade based on two-factors, two (homogeneous) goods Heckscher-Ohlin models. Usually, one distinguishes

---

[1] The theory of product cycles (Vernon, 1987, 1966; Hirsch, 1967; Gandolfo, 1986, ch.8.5) suggests an explanation for a shift of production sites and sales areas due to the life cycle of a product. Initially developed, produced and consumed in an advanced country, sales and then production of a good move towards other countries, first to other advanced ones, then to developing countries, where, at the end of the product cycle, all production takes place. The basic mechanisms of TPR is independent of foreign direct investment and the life cycle of goods but relies on a relative change of factor endowment which is a result of the accumulation process of production factors.

between two possible outcomes of free trade: Either factor prices are equalized and both countries are incompletely specialized or at least one country is completely specialized and no factor-price equalization obtains. In contrast, with differing time preference rates and at least one differentiated good, a situation of incomplete specialization and different factor rewards will result. This model generates trade patterns which depend on the relative factor endowment of the trading partners. Since no accumulation processes (apart from extending the varieties) is included, trade patterns will not change over time.

The analysis of the world economy in chapter 3 is restricted to the balanced growth path, a standard approach in the literature. With respect to convergence, however, it is interesting to know whether countries will ever reach a balanced growth path (BGP) and, related to this question, what happens if they are pushed off the BGP. This is the question tackled in chapter 4 "Transitional dynamics, convergence and international capital flows in two-country models of innovation and growth". The chapter investigates explicitly the stability of the BGP for a Grossman-Helpman type model (a two-country version of Grossman and Helpman, 1991a, ch. 3.2), and proves, by using the Mulligan and Sala-i-Martin (1993) approach, that it is locally saddle path stable. We further derive analytically global behaviour and study international capital flows during the adjustment period.

In the subsequent chapter, a first step is undertaken to allow for changing trade relations. International perfect spillovers of knowledge lead to an automatic equalization of growth rates. Chapter 5 "Impatience, factor endowment and trade patterns in a small open economy of endogenous growth", therefore, restricts knowledge flows to the home economy and introduces endogenous technological change by modelling differentiated goods as middle goods, generalizing Grossman and Helpman (1991a, ch. 6). In such a context, physical factor richness no longer predicts trade patterns in a reliable way, even if countries differ only in their factor endowment. Further, if the consumers' time preference rates are allowed to vary between countries, they influence trade patterns, too. Thus the interaction of factor endowment and time preference can easily lead to a situation where a physically capital rich country imports the capital intensive good. Technological progress in this model favours both primary factors to the same extent, thus Ricardian effects have no influence on trade patterns. Another interesting aspect, however, the question of "catching up, falling behind, and forging ahead" as called by Abramovitz (1986), can be accounted for by the model. We find that a country which is more concerned about its future, or about future generations, which translates into a lower time preference rate, will experience, ceteris paribus, a higher growth rate than other countries. Thus consumption per capita of this country can overtake consumption in other countries.

Chapter 6 "Trade pattern reversal: The role of technological change, factor accumulation and government intervention" finally, gives some theoretical explanations for TPR. Possible reasons for such a situation to arise are investigated in a model which contains Ricardian and Heckscher-Ohlin features by combining models of Grossman and Helpman (1991a, ch.8), Lucas (1988) and Ethier (1982). Trade patterns are no longer influenced only by factor endowment, but also by technological differences by allowing, in contrast to chapter 5, an asymmetrical effect of technological progress on factors. In such a situation, a change of technological leadership can lead to a reversal of trade patterns. In addition, the role of government intervention on factor accumulation and technological change is studied. It turns out, that this provides an alternative explanation for TPR. The conclusion mentions the implications concerning convergence and divergence of countries. Finally, the very last paragraph takes up the conjecture from the beginning about impatience and completes the chapter by mentioning that the preceding analysis implies that different time preference rates are indeed one way to explain catching-up processes and reversals of trade patterns.

2. Basic concepts of the "new" growth theory

After having described the scope of the study, we now present some basic concepts and assumptions employed by the "new" growth theory. The presentation is based on Grossman and Helpman (1991a), though similar (if not to say identical) concepts are used in other parts of the literature on endogenous growth (Romer, 1986, 1990; Lucas, 1988; Rivera-Batiz and Romer, 1991).

Consumption side

The basic framework for modelling the consumption side is provided by the concept of a representative household. Neglecting distributional effects, all households in one economy are regarded to be identical such that all relevant economic information can be observed by looking at the behaviour of one household only. This representative household is endowed with a certain quantity of production factors and owns some financial wealth.

Production factors are, e.g., unskilled labour or human capital. A household can possess both labour and human capital. Human capital is a set of specialized skills which can be acquired by taking part in education activities (e.g. schools). Though it is sometimes argued that it cannot be easily imagined how households can offer both human capital and unskilled labour at the same time, this is a frequent assumption in the literature. This approach can be justified by arguing that households, on the micro level, possess either human capital or unskilled labour, and thus are not really homogenous, but the macro level can be described with sufficient accuracy by taking a household with both types of education levels as representative. Another, more model consistent interpretation is to say that households consist of several individuals (which fits very well to the term cohorts or dynasties) and the ratio of human capital to unskilled labour in each household is identical.

Physical capital plays a minor role in those models, since the scope is to highlight the importance of intentional R&D activities of firms. Of course, this has often been attacked, but physical capital can be included into the models (e.g. Grossman and Helpman, 1991a, ch. 5). Other basic models of the literature of endogenous growth do include physical capital (e.g., Romer, 1986; Lucas, 1988; Romer, 1990; Barro, 1990). It is interesting to note that the concept of capital in some of these models, (e.g., Romer 1990) differs slightly from the "traditional" one. Capital is no longer viewed as a homogenous good but as consisting of a multitude of differentiated capital goods. This allows to represent the accumulation of capital as a process which increases the available range of differentiated capital goods.

In addition to production factors, households can accumulate, by saving, financial wealth in the form of shares in firms. Often in these models, the production side is characterized by monopolistic competition which implies that firms have a certain value, equivalent, in a perfect foresight equilibrium, to the discounted sum of future current profits. On the aggregate level, financial wealth of all consumers equals the value of all firms producing in the economy.

Being in a dynamic framework, some words have to be said about the process of expectation formation. Agents are assumed to have rational expectations, which, in the absence of uncertainty, amounts to perfect foresight. This is hard to believe and should not be taken too literally but rather be seen as a way of modelling a behaviour which is characterized by learning. If agents form expectations about future events (timepaths of prices, etc.) by using past information, they do learn, after some time, the true structure of the economy (the true model) and are then able to predict the consequence of their actions. Thus they can form their expectations in consistence with the model; agents have perfect foresight.

The static part of consumption behaviour is characterized by preferences which are either of the Cobb-Douglas type in the case of two homogenous final goods or of the Dixit-Stiglitz type if one (the) final good is differentiated. Cobb-Douglas type demand means that final goods are imperfect substitutes with an elasticity of substitution of one and that expenditure for one good is a constant fraction of consumers' total expenditure. In the case of Dixit-Stiglitz preferences the elasticity of substitution between varieties is greater than unity and demand for each of them depends on the price of the other varieties. These two concepts can be combined by constructing a two-level utility function. On the first level, a Cobb-Douglas type utility function for two final goods is specified. On the sub-utility level – utility resulting from the consumption of one good – a Dixit-Stiglitz formulation is used.

Production side

The standard production side of Grossman-Helpman models consists of a model of monopolistic competition. Each firm produces one specific variety of a final good under constant returns to scale. Due to the demand structure, a firm has some monopoly power and can therefore charge a profit maximizing price which lies above marginal costs. These current profits can be used to finance up-front costs of R&D, necessary to produce a blueprint for a new variety. Each firm which enters the economy first develops new blueprint (and does not copy from other firms) due to assumption of perfect patent protection. In addition, it would be unreasonable for a firm to develop an already existing variety since it would then have to share the market with the other firm.

The cash flow *CF* of a typical firm in a monopolistic competition framework with a positive innovation rate is as represented in figure 1.1.

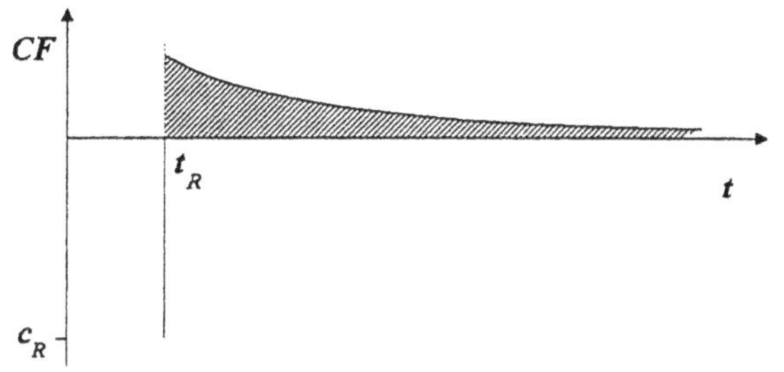

Figure 1.1: The cash flow of a firm in a monopolistic competition setting

At the beginning, firms take a loan, granted by households, to cover R&D costs c_R. Then, by producing and selling their variety, they make profits π. Profits fall if the number of competitors increases. Allowing for free entry and exit, the sum of all future current profits a firm receives during its lifetime (the hatched area), discounted at a discount factor $D(\tau)$, is equal to the R&D costs c_R:

$$c_R = \int_{t_R}^{\infty} D(\tau)\pi(\tau)d\tau.$$

Thus, in the present-value sense, firms make no profits (pure profits are excluded) due to the free-entry assumption, current profits, however, can (and have to) be made, since firms must service their debt resulting from R&D expenses.

The mechanism which leads to positive long-run growth rates is due to the assumption of a public stock of knowledge which is used *and* created by R&D activities. The development of dn new blueprints requires the employment of some factors L (read this as "number of engineers") for a certain period of time dt and uses the stock of knowledge Kn available in the economy; $dn = L\,Kn\,dt$[2]. Now, if

2 The "number" of varieties is given by the measure n which is treated as a continuous variable. The advantage is that integer constraints for n can be neglected. Thus, strictly speaking, one should not think of a countable quantity but rather of a multitude or a set of varieties. In the following chapters we will nevertheless speak about the (measure of the) number of varieties,

knowledge increases linearly in n, the rate of development of new goods is found by simple rearrangement; $\dot{n}/n = L$. This is exactly the Grossman-Helpman approach (going back to Romer, 1990). The growth rate of the economy is then, depending on the definition, either, e.g., the rate of innovation of new goods, or the rate of growth of a suitably defined GNP which is identical to the rate of growth of per-capita income, given that in this model the population does not grow. In the model presented below, the growth rate is the rate at which new varieties are introduced in the economy. Consumers benefit from growth through a widening of the range of final goods they can consume, though neither income increases, nor prices for final goods decrease. Thus it would be appropriate to talk about endogenous "development" or "expansion". If, however, varieties are used as intermediate goods (as, e.g., in chapter 5 and 6), growth can indeed be understood as growth of GNP and thus of per-capita consumption.

Interaction

Combining consumption and production sides by market equilibria leads to a closed economy model with positive long-run growth rates. Consumers supply their factors of production which are employed by firms. Furthermore, final output supplied by firms is consumed by households which also supply their savings used by firms to finance R&D.

A simple model explaining some basic mechanisms is the one developed by Grossman and Helpman (1991a, ch. 3.2). A quasi-reduced form of the model[3] consists of an optimality condition for the allocation of expenditure E over time as a function of the interest rate r and the time preference rate ρ,

$$\frac{\dot{E}}{E} = r - \rho, \tag{1}$$

a full-employment condition for the only resource, labour L, where the number of firms is given by n, the value of each firm is v, θ is a preference parameter (the elasticity of substitution between two varieties is given by $\varepsilon = 1/(1-\theta)$),

$$\frac{\dot{n}}{n} + \frac{\theta}{vn} E = L, \tag{2}$$

since, on the one hand, this facilitates the mode of expression without, one the other hand, violating mathematical correctness too much.

3 Cf. Grossman and Helpman (1991a, ch. 3.2.) or chapter 3 - in a two-country version - for a detailed description of the model.

an asset or financial capital market equilibrium condition, determining the interest rate,

$$\pi + \dot{v} = rv, \tag{3}$$

where profits of firms are given by $\pi = \frac{1-\theta}{n}E$, and a flow budget constraint of the economy,

$$E + \dot{A} = r\,A + wL, \tag{4}$$

where A is the value of assets of all households and w stands for the wage rate. Since the value of firms equals the value of assets, $A = nv$. In equilibrium, wages are given by $w = vn$. A dot indicates the derivative with respect to time.

It can now be easily shown (see e.g. appendix of chapter 4), that the budget constraint (4) is always fulfilled, given equations (1) - (3), which reflects Walras' Law. Thus the model can be analyzed using equations (1) - (3) only and we can choose the timepath of one variable as numeraire. Grossman and Helpman took total expenditure E as numeraire, which implies that on the balanced growth path factor rewards, prices and the total asset value A are constant. The reduced form of the model then reads (note that $r = \rho$),

$$\dot{n} = n\,L - \theta v^{-1}, \quad \dot{v} = \rho v - (1-\theta)n^{-1}. \tag{R}$$ [4]

A note concerning the determination of the interest rate is in order, here. The usual Grossman-Helpman argument runs as follows. Equation (3) is a no-arbitrage condition for the financial capital market which states that consumers would invest financial capital of value v in firms only if the return, given by profits π and capital gains (or losses) $\dot{v}$ equals the return of a same amount invested in a risk-less loan yielding interest rate r. This argument might not seem very convincing, given that in this model there is no one offering a riskless investment opportunity. One can argue, however, that consumers can grant consumption loans (Grossman and Helpman, 1991a, ch.2); since this is not explicitly modelled, and, above all, consumers would not indebt themselves, given that they are all by assumption

4 Alternatively, we could choose the price of a differentiated good (or any other price) as numeraire; the reduced form then becomes $\dot{n} = nL - nE$, $\dot{E}/E = E\,\theta^{-1} - L - \rho$. As it must turn out, analyzing this reduced form further leads to the same results as we will give below for the reduced form (R), i.e. same rate of growth, real price for the final good, factor reward and interest rate $r = \rho$.

identical, this is not very convincing, either. Another interpretation is that the interest rate reflects the value financial capital has for firms: The interests they pay on capital invested equals the sum of dividend rate and rate of capital gains (or losses),

$$r = \frac{\pi}{v} + \frac{\dot{v}}{v}.$$

An explanation for the interest rate, based on the supply side for financial capital is as follows: Consumers hold shares in firms of value nv. Each period they receive profits, which equals the change of the value of their share holdings due to the increase of the number of firms, $v\dot{n} = \pi n$. Adding on both sides fictitious incomes (or losses) due to capital gains, one obtains $v\dot{n} + \dot{v}n = \pi n + \dot{v}n$ which reads, after dividing by nv,

$$\frac{\dot{n}}{n} + \frac{\dot{v}}{v} = \frac{\pi}{v} + \frac{\dot{v}}{v}.$$

Since the value of total financial capital invested is $A = nv$, this reads

$$\frac{\dot{A}}{A} = \frac{\pi}{v} + \frac{\dot{v}}{v}.$$

Defining the interest rate as the rate of increase of wealth A over time, we find

$$r = \frac{\pi}{v} + \frac{\dot{v}}{v},$$

which is the "capital-market no-arbitrage condition".

Saddle path

We now turn to the question of how to solve the reduced system (R). In order to find out, how consumer choose the "right" initial value for the v and how the balanced growth path of the economy looks like, we draw a phase diagram of these equations.

The zero-motion lines are determined by setting the above equations equal to zero and solving for v. The line for $\dot{v}/v = 0$ lies above the one for $\dot{n}/n = 0$ only if the economy is sufficiently large to sustain long-run positive growth rates, i.e. $(1-\theta)L > \theta\rho$. The straight arrows in the (v,n)-plane indicate the direction of motion of v and n above, below and in between the zero-motion loci.

Equipped with this graphical tool, we can now determine the equilibrium trajectory. Assume that the historically given quantity of differentiated goods is given by n_0. Then the initial value for v has to be chosen in order to determine

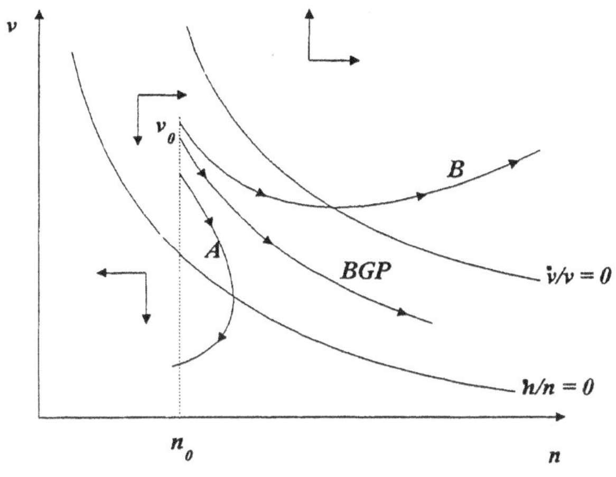

Figure 1.2: The closed economy phase diagram

the "next" n and v, thus consumers decide only once which value to choose for v and from then on, the evolution of the economy is completely determined by equations (R). If agents decided to value firms lower than v_0, then the economies evolution is determined by path A. First, the number of differentiated goods increases, then comes to a halt and finally decreases. Eventually it will hit the n- and/ or v-axis and will then be negative. Clearly, this cannot be optimal and, from an economic point of view, makes no sense since the value of the representative firm would become negative, too[5]. Similarly for any value above v_0: The number of firms would increase *and* the value of the firms would increase which cannot be optimal since after some time, the consumers budget constraint would no longer be satisfied but total wealth would exceed total expenditure. Such a path is characterized by "bubbles" in the firm value. The only path which satisfies all optimality conditions is the balanced growth path, denoted by BGP. Thus forward-looking agents choose the "right" (in the sense of optimal) initial value v_0, the economy jumps on the saddle path BGP.

[5] Of course, this is no rigorous proof. See the appendix of chapter 2, Infinite horizon maximization I, for more details.

Stationary state vs. balanced growth path

The last subsection has shown that the only reasonable solution of the model (i.e. the only economic reasonable behaviour of agents) is characterized by a balanced growth path. We will now formally describe its properties and then briefly compare this solution to another one, frequently encountered in dynamic models.

A balanced growth path is a solution to a dynamic equation system where some variables grow at a constant rate. By looking at the budget constraint (4) it becomes clear why this is the only "balanced" solution to the model: Replacing wages by the equilibrium condition $w = vn = A$, the budget constraint can be written as $\dot{A} = (\rho + L)A - E$. This implies, since total expenditure E is constant, that the value of assets (which equals the value of all firms in the economy) either increases or decreases continuously. In such a situation, neither factor rewards, nor goods prices are constant (and neither approach a constant). Therefore, in order to avoid to be on an unstable arm as depicted in figure 1.2, the value of assets must be constant at all times. Hence, the balanced growth path is characterized by constant wages, prices and total asset value A and a constant growth rate which can then be obtained from the reduced form (R). Since the value of all assets is constant, the number of differentiated goods must increase at the same rate g, $\dot{n}/n = g$, as the value of the representative firm falls, $\dot{v}/v = -g$. Then, system (R) can be written as

$$g = L - \theta(vn)^{-1}, \qquad -g = \rho - (1-\theta)(vn)^{-1}.$$

The dynamic equation system has become a static one, which can be solved for the growth rate g and nv, the total quantity of wealth in the economy. It turns out that the growth rate is $g = (1-\theta)L - \theta\rho$, i.e. new varieties are introduced at that rate. Clearly, this rate is positive only if consumers are not too impatient (ρ is too large) given the size of the country. Too high a time preference rate means that consumers request very high interest rates for their financial capital. If firms cannot pay these interest rates, because profits are too low, no investment would take place and the economy would remain in a stationary state.

If, on the other hand, we did not include into the model a public stock of knowledge, equal to the number of varieties, the reduced form of the model would read (as in Grossman and Helpman, 1991a, ch. 3.1)

$$\dot{n} = L - \theta/v, \qquad \dot{v} = \rho v - (1-\theta)/n.$$

Again, in trying to find a solution, we would proceed as above: Set all equations of motion to zero and draw a phase diagram. With the help of that diagram[6] we would again determine the optimal initial value for v. What differs from the analysis of the reduced model (R), however, is the solution: We do no longer find a balanced growth path but a stationary state, which means that all variables (n and v) are constant. Setting the reduced form equal to zero gives $v^* = \theta/L$ and $n^* = (1-\theta)/(\rho v^*)$ and we obtain as stationary state solution

$$\left(n^*, v^*\right) = \left(\frac{1-\theta}{\theta}\frac{L}{\rho}, \frac{\theta}{L}\right).$$

Thus, the model no longer predicts growth in the sense of a continuous extension of the number of varieties but growth comes to a halt.

6 The diagram can be found in Grossman and Helpman (1991a, p. 56).

*Chapter 2: On an additional condition for factor-price equalization in intertemporal Heckscher-Ohlin models**

1. Introduction

The pure theory of international trade based on two homogenous goods, two factors, two countries Heckscher-Ohlin models distinguishes between two possible outcomes of international trade: Either factor prices are equalized and both countries are incompletely specialized or at least one country is completely specialized and no factor-price equalization obtains. The assumptions necessary for factor-price equalization (FPE) are free trade, absence of trade impediments including transportation costs, that both countries produce with the same technology and the absence of factor-intensity reversal. Taking into consideration models combining the Heckscher-Ohlin approach with endogenous growth (see, e.g. Grossman and Helpman, 1991a, ch.7, Dinopoulos et.al., 1993) one becomes aware of the fact that in an intertemporal context, another condition adds to the one mentioned above: Individual discount rates must not differ between countries.
In the following, this effect is demonstrated in, what we believe, the simplest possible way by using a slightly modified version of the Grossman and Helpman (1989) model. The modification consists of fixing the numbers of factors to two and in assuming fixed R&D costs (see e.g. Barro and Sala-i-Martin, 1992). Please note that the effect presented does not depend on these simplifications but arises in models with positive long-run growth rates and more sophisticated R&D specifications, too (cf. Chapter 3).
In the first section the two-country model will be sketched. The second section will prove the main proposition before final remarks conclude the chapter.

---

* Slightly modified version of Wälde (1994a).

2. A two-country world

The consumer side is modelled by using the concept of a representative household which maximizes utility over an infinite horizon. The utility function is given by

$$U^i(t)=\int_t^\infty \exp\left[-\rho^i(\tau-t)\right]\left(\frac{\sigma}{\theta}\log\int_o^n x_c(j)^\theta dj+(1-\sigma)\log Z_c\right)d\tau,\ 0<\theta,\sigma<1, \qquad (1)$$

where ρ^i is the individual discount rate of consumers (with $i = A, B$ indicating the country) and $n = n^A + n^B$ is the measure for the number of varieties available for consumption. With these preferences both representative consumers (one in each country) devote a fraction σ of their spending E^i to the differentiated good and the remaining fraction 1-σ to the homogeneous good. This allows us first to derive static demand functions, insert them into the utility function (1) and then maximize it with respect to expenditure subject to an intertemporal budget constraint to derive an optimal allocation of expenditure over time. We further know that since all firms have the same production function and, independently of the *sector*, pay the same factor rewards, all varieties produced in *one* country are equally priced. All of this gives (cf. appendix) aggregate demand functions for the differentiated good of the form

$$x^i=\frac{\left(p_x^i\right)^{-\varepsilon}}{n^A\left(p_x^A\right)^{1-\varepsilon}+n^B\left(p_x^B\right)^{1-\varepsilon}}\sigma\left(E^A+E^B\right), \qquad (2)$$

where the elasticity of substitution between any two varieties is given by $\varepsilon = 1/(1-\theta)$, and for the homogeneous good

$$Z^A+Z^B=\frac{1-\sigma}{p_Z}\left(E^A+E^B\right). \qquad (3)$$

The intertemporal allocation of expenditure follows (cf. appendix)

$$\frac{\dot{E}^i}{E^i}=r^i-\rho^i. \qquad (4)$$

Both countries are endowed with labour and human capital and consist of two manufacturing sectors, each one employing both factors for producing one homogeneous good (food) and one differentiated final good. The sectors can be ranked by their factor intensity, with the sector producing the differentiated good being the more human capital intensive one. Perfect competition in the food industry Z implies

$$p_Z = c_Z\left(w_L^i, w_H^i\right), \tag{5}$$

where $c_Z\left(w_L^i, w_H^i\right)$ is the unit cost function for good Z depending on factor rewards, w_L^i and w_H^i, for labour and human capital, whereas manufacturers of the differentiated products practice mark-up pricing (cf. appendix):

$$p_x^i = \frac{1}{\theta} c_x\left(w_L^i, w_H^i\right). \tag{6}$$

Prior to producing a differentiated good a new variety has to be developed which requires fixed costs ϕ which do not differ between countries[1]. Allowing for free entry and exit, an equilibrium will be characterized by an equalization of R&D costs and the discounted sum of future current profits $\pi^i(\tau)$:

$$\phi = \int_t^\infty \exp\left[-\left(R(\tau) - R(t)\right)\right]\pi^i(\tau)d\tau. \tag{7}$$

The discount factor is given by $R(s) = \int_o^s r(u)du$, where $r(u)$ is the interest rate at time u.

Finally we have to specify factor market clearing conditions. The supply of factors is assumed to be totally inelastic, the unit demand functions for factors result from cost minimization and the application of Shephard's lemma. With the assumption that factor rewards adjust such that markets clear at every moment in time we obtain

$$a_{LX}\left(w_L^i, w_H^i\right)n^i x^i + a_{LZ}\left(w_L^i, w_H^i\right)Z^i = L^i, \tag{8}$$

$$a_{HX}\left(w_L^i, w_H^i\right)n^i x^i + a_{HZ}\left(w_L^i, w_H^i\right)Z^i = H^i.$$

Thus the model turns out to be similar to the Helpman and Krugman (1985, ch.7) model where the static zero-profit condition is replaced by an intertemporal one and the utility maximization calculation of the consumers is enlarged by an intertemporal component. The model can be solved for equilibrium prices, output and the number of varieties by using equation (2), (3), (5) - (8) with total expenditure $E^A + E^B$ chosen as numeraire.

---

1 The R&D process is modelled to require no factors of production (or else a third (specific) factor) since this simplifies the proof of the main proposition. See chapter 2 for a more "natural" R&D process.

3. Unequal factor rewards and incomplete specialization

Differentiating (7) with respect to time (cf. appendix) yields the usual capital market no-arbitrage conditions which express the indifference of agents between a riskless loan or buying a share of a firm,

$$\pi^i = r^i \phi . \tag{9}$$

With equation (6) and (2) current profits are

$$\pi^i = \left(p_x^i - c_x\left(w_L^i, w_H^i\right)\right)x^i = \left(p_x^i\right)^{1-\varepsilon} \frac{(1-\theta)\sigma\left(E^A + E^B\right)}{n^A\left(p_x^A\right)^{1-\varepsilon} + n^B\left(p_x^B\right)^{1-\varepsilon}} . \tag{10}$$

By subtracting equation (9) from itself ($i = A, B$) we find

$$\left(\left(p_x^A\right)^{1-\varepsilon} - \left(p_x^B\right)^{1-\varepsilon}\right)\frac{(1-\theta)\sigma\left(E^A + E^B\right)}{n^A\left(p_x^A\right)^{1-\varepsilon} + n^B\left(p_x^B\right)^{1-\varepsilon}} = \left(r^A - r^B\right)\phi . \tag{11}$$

We know that factor-price equalization requires equalization of goods prices due to the one-to-one mapping between goods prices and factor rewards given by the pricing equations (5) and (6) under the assumption of no factor-intensity reversal. Thus if prices for the differentiated goods differ, factor prices cannot be equalized. Equation (11), however, tells us that prices for the differentiated good are equalized only if interest rates are equalized. In an equilibrium, however, expenditure of every country is constant and thus via (4) a country's interest rate has to equal its time preference rate. Now, if these rates differ, goods prices for the differentiated good differ and consequently factor prices do not equalize.

What remains to be shown is under which conditions both countries are incompletely specialized in the long-run equilibrium. These conditions can be easily derived from the factor-market clearing conditions: Rewrite them as $L_X^i + L_Z^i = L^i$ and $h_X^i L_X^i + h_Z^i L_Z^i = H^i$ where h_X^i and h_Z^i are the human capital intensities in sector X and Z, respectively. Solving for L_X^i and L_Z^i gives the usual conditions for incomplete specialization: If the factor endowment of the country i lies within a certain cone of diversification whose boundaries are given by $h_Z^i L^i < H^i < h_X^i L^i$, then both L_X^i and L_Z^i are positive. Consequently H_X^i and H_Z^i are positive, too, and country i is incompletely specialized. Therefore, as long as individual discount rates differ and both countries lie within the cone of diversification, both countries produce both goods, but factor prices differ.

4. Conclusion

In static free trade models with two homogenous goods and two factors, FPE results if both countries are not too dissimilarily endowed, factor-intensity reversal is excluded, production takes place with identical technologies and transportation costs are neglected. Dynamic models further require identical individual discount rates. If discount rates differ between countries and at least one final good is heterogeneous, factor prices can not be equalized even if both countries produce both goods.

Finally we add that, since unequal discount rates imply unequal interest rates, we obtain an equilibrium only under the assumption of internationally immobile financial capital. The consequences of an international mobility of capital are studied in the next chapter.

Appendix

1. Continuous time discounting: Deriving equation (1)

We derive continuous time discounting factors as used in equation (1). (This follows the hints by Feichtinger and Hartl, 1986, p.12.)

The present value *PV* of an amount x we receive in one period is $PV=(1+i)^{-1}x$ where i is the effective rate of interest, i.e. the annual percentage rate. If interest is paid n times a year at the rate of r/n per period, the annual percentage rate is (Berck and Sydsaeter, 1991, p. 135) $i=(1+r/n)^n-1$. Thus the *PV* of x is $PV=(1+r/n)^{-n}x$. Now if interest rates are charged at every moment in time $(n\to\infty)$ then the annual percentage rate is $i=\lim_{n\to\infty}(1+r/n)^n-1=\exp[r]-1$.[2] Consequently $PV=\exp[-r]x$. In an analogous way the *PV* of an amount x we receive in τ periods is $(1+i)^{-\tau}x$ and with continuous discounting the *PV* is $PV=\exp[-r\tau]x$. Calculating the $PV(t)$ of an income stream $x(\tau)$ at time t then

2 To illustrate this equation assume an annual interest rate of $i=0{,}1\mathrel{\hat{=}}10\%$. The equivalent value for r is then given by $r=\ln(i+1)=\ln(1{,}1)\approx 0{,}095\mathrel{\hat{=}}9{,}5\%$.

simply requires to sum up all future discounted amounts $x(\tau)$ which yields $PV(t)=\int_t^\infty \exp[-r(\tau-t)]x(\tau)d\tau$.

If the interest rate r is a function of time the discount factor $\exp[-r\tau]$ becomes $\exp\left[-\int_0^\tau r(s)ds\right]$.

2. Static utility maximization: Deriving equation (2)

Here we derive utility maximizing demand functions. Since the behaviour of agents is independent of the country they are living in, we neglect the country index. The problem consists in

$$\max_{x(i),Z} u(\tau)=\left(\int_0^n x(i)^\theta di\right)^{\frac{\sigma}{\theta}} Z^{1-\sigma}, \quad \text{s.t. } \int_0^n p(i)x(i)di+p_Z Z\le E(\tau),$$

with $0<\theta,\sigma<1$; $p(i),p_Z,E(\tau),n\in R^+$.

A two step maximization is undertaken (used e.g. by Dixit and Stiglitz, 1977 and Helpman and Krugman, 1985, ch. 6). First total expenditure $E(\tau)$ is partitioned between sectors Z and X and then the fraction of $E(\tau)$ for sector X is partitioned between varieties produced in this sector.

First step

$$\max_{X,Z} u(\tau)=X^\sigma Z^{1-\sigma}, \quad \text{s.t. } p_X X+p_Z Z=E(\tau).$$

The result is

$$X=\frac{\sigma E(\tau)}{p_X}, \quad Z=\frac{(1-\sigma)E(\tau)}{p_Z}.$$

Second step

$$\max_{x(i)} X=\left(\int_0^n x(i)^\theta di\right)^{\frac{1}{\theta}}, \qquad \text{s.t. } \int_0^n p(i)x(i)di\le \sigma E(\tau).$$

The Lagrangean is

$$\mathcal{L}=\left(\int_0^n x(i)^\theta di\right)^{\frac{1}{\theta}}+\lambda\left(\sigma E(\tau)-\int_0^n p(i)x(i)di\right).$$

The first order conditions are the budget constraint and

$$\frac{1}{\theta}\left(\int_0^n x(i)^\theta di\right)^{\frac{1}{\theta}-1}\theta x(i)^{\theta-1}-\lambda p(i)=0 \Leftrightarrow \frac{\left(\int_0^n x(i)^\theta di\right)^{\frac{1}{\theta}}}{\int_0^n x(i)^\theta di}x(i)^{\theta-1}=\lambda p(i).$$

By reinserting X we obtain

$$X^{1-\theta}x(i)^{\theta-1}=\lambda p(i)\Leftrightarrow X\lambda^{\frac{-1}{1-\theta}}=x(i)p(i)^{\frac{1}{1-\theta}},$$

which means that since the LHS of the last equation is a constant, i.e. is independent of the integration variable di, the right hand side is a constant, too (Grossman and Helpman, 1991a, p.46, footnote 2). This fact can be used to pull this product outside the integral in the budget constraint and we find with $\varepsilon=1/(1-\theta)$

$$\int_0^n p(i)^\varepsilon p(i)^{1-\varepsilon}x(i)di\le\sigma E(\tau)\Leftrightarrow p(i)^\varepsilon x(i)\int_0^n p(i)^{1-\varepsilon}di\le\sigma E(\tau).$$

Solving for $x(i)$ then finally yields the demand function

$$x(i)=\frac{p(i)^{-\varepsilon}}{\int_0^n p(i)^{1-\varepsilon}di}\sigma E(\tau),\qquad \varepsilon=1/(1-\theta).$$

With $n=n^A+n^B$ we obtain

$$x(i)=\frac{p(i)^{-\varepsilon}}{\int_0^n p(i)^{1-\varepsilon}di}\sigma E(\tau)=\frac{p(i)^{-\varepsilon}}{\int_0^{n^A}p(i)^{1-\varepsilon}di+\int_{n^A}^{n^A+n^B}p(i)^{1-\varepsilon}di}\sigma E(\tau).$$

Since all varieties coming from one country are equally priced we find equation (2)

$$x^i=\frac{\left(p_x^i\right)^{-\varepsilon}}{n^A\left(p_x^A\right)^{1-\varepsilon}+n^B\left(p_x^B\right)^{1-\varepsilon}}\sigma E(\tau).$$

3. Optimal allocation of expenditure over time: Deriving equation (4)

Maximize the intertemporal utility function $U(t)$

$$U(t)=\int_t^\infty \exp[-\rho(\tau-t)]\log u(\tau)d\tau,\quad \rho>0,$$

where $u(\tau)$ is the instantaneous utility function $u(\tau)=\left(\int_0^n x(i)^\theta di\right)^{\frac{\sigma}{\theta}}Z^{1-\sigma}$, $0<\theta,\sigma<1$, subject to the budget constraint (BC)[3]

[3] This follows the sparse indications by Grossman and Helpman (1989, p.1265, footnote 4).

$$\int_t^\infty \exp\left[-\left(R(\tau)-R(t)\right)\right]E(\tau)d\tau = \int_t^\infty \exp\left[-\left(R(\tau)-R(t)\right)\right]I(\tau)d\tau + n(t)v(t),$$

where $R(u) = \int_0^u r(s)ds$ is the discount factor depending on the interest rate $r(s)$. The LHS of the BC is the discounted sum of future expenditure which must equal the sum of discounted future income $I(\tau)$ plus the current value of assets held by the consumer $n(t)v(t)$.

The maximization procedure first derives the static indirect utility function and inserts it into the dynamic utility function. Then this dynamic indirect utility function is maximized with respect to total expenditure $E(\tau)$. It results an equation determining the optimal intertemporal allocation of expenditure.

Indirect utility function

In order to derive the indirect utility function we use the results obtained from the static maximization procedure. By inserting demand functions into the instantaneous utility function we obtain the indirect utility function $u_{ind.}(\tau)$:

$$u_{ind.}(\tau) = \left(\int_0^n x(i)^\theta di\right)^{\frac{\sigma}{\theta}} Z^{1-\sigma} = \left(\int_0^n \left(\frac{p(i)^{-\varepsilon}}{\int_0^n p(i)^{1-\varepsilon} di}\sigma E(\tau)\right)^\theta di\right)^{\frac{\sigma}{\theta}} \left(\frac{(1-\sigma)E(\tau)}{p_Z}\right)^{1-\sigma}$$

$$= \left(\int_0^n \left(\frac{p(i)^{-\varepsilon}}{\int_0^n p(i)^{1-\varepsilon} di}\sigma\right)^\theta di\right)^{\frac{\sigma}{\theta}} \left(\frac{(1-\sigma)}{p_Y}\right)^{1-\sigma} E(\tau) =: P(\tau)E(\tau).$$

Maximization of the dynamic indirect utility function

Now the indirect utility function is inserted into the intertemporal utility function,

$$U(t) = \int_t^\infty \exp\left[-\rho(\tau-t)\right]\log u_{ind.}(\tau)d\tau = \int_t^\infty \exp\left[-\rho(\tau-t)\right]\left(\log E(\tau) + \log P(\tau)\right)d\tau.$$

Maximize this expression with respect to $E(\tau)$ subject to the budget constraint

$$\int_t^\infty \exp\left[-\left(R(\tau)-R(t)\right)\right]E(\tau)d\tau = \int_t^\infty \exp\left[-\left(R(\tau)-R(t)\right)\right]I(\tau)d\tau + n(t)v(t). \quad \text{(A.1)}$$

We build the Lagrangean with λ as the time-independent Lagrange multiplier

$$\mathcal{L} = \int_t^\infty \exp\left[-\rho(\tau-t)\right]\left(\log E(\tau) + \log P(\tau)\right)d\tau$$
$$-\lambda\left(\int_t^\infty \exp\left[-\left(R(\tau)-R(t)\right)\right]E(\tau)d\tau - \int_t^\infty \exp\left[-\left(R(\tau)-R(t)\right)\right]I(\tau)d\tau - n(t)v(t)\right),$$

whose first order conditions are (A.1) and

$$\mathcal{L}_{E(\tau)} = \exp[-\rho(\tau-t)]\frac{1}{E(\tau)} - \lambda\exp[-(R(\tau)-R(t))] = 0 \Leftrightarrow$$

$$\frac{\exp[-\rho(\tau-t)]}{E(\tau)} = \lambda\exp[-(R(\tau)-R(t))] \Leftrightarrow \exp[R(\tau)-R(t)-\rho(\tau-t)] = \lambda E(\tau) \Leftrightarrow$$

$$R(\tau)-R(t)-\rho(\tau-t) = \log\lambda + \log E(\tau).$$

Differentiating with respect to time τ gives

$$\frac{\dot{E}(\tau)}{E(\tau)} = \dot{R}(\tau)-\rho.$$

With R as discount factor expressed by $R(\tau)=\int_0^\tau r(s)ds$ we can express $\dot{R}(\tau)$ as $\dot{R}(\tau)=r(\tau)-\int_0^\tau \frac{\partial}{\partial\tau}r(s)ds = r(\tau)$ and thus

$$\frac{\dot{E}(\tau)}{E(\tau)} = r(\tau)-\rho.$$

Often in Grossman-Helpman type models, the interest rate is given by the time preference rate, $r(\tau)=\rho$ (e.g. by normalizing expenditure at unity). Then the discount factor becomes

$$R(s)=\int_0^s r(u)du = \rho\int_0^s du = \rho s.$$

4. Mark-up pricing: Deriving equation (6)

Profits of a firm producing a variety k are given by $\pi^k = p_x^k(x^k)x^k - c(x^k)$. The crucial difference to modelling a perfectly competitive behaviour of firms is that firms are not price takers but influence the price of their goods by the quantity they sell. In contrast to a monopoly, however, firms do compete with other firms which produce similar goods which are imperfect substitutes. The profit maximizing output quantity is determined by (second order conditions are assumed to hold)

$$\frac{\partial\pi^k}{\partial x^k} = p_x^k(x^k) + \frac{\partial p_x^k(x^k)}{\partial x^k}x^k - \frac{\partial c(x^k)}{\partial x^k} = 0.$$

Assuming a cost-function which is linear in output x^k and rearranging gives

$$p_x^k(x^k)\left(1+\frac{\partial p_x^k(x^k)}{\partial x^k}\frac{x^k}{p_x^k(x^k)}\right)=c,$$

where c are unit costs. Defining $\varepsilon=-\frac{\partial x^k}{\partial p_x^k(x^k)}\frac{p_x^k(x^k)}{x^k}$ as the price elasticity of demand, this reads $p_x^k(x^k)=\frac{c}{1-1/\varepsilon}$. Since the price elasticity of demand is given by $\varepsilon=1/(1-\theta)$, the profit maximizing output is implicitly given by $p_x^k(x^k)=\frac{c}{1-1/\varepsilon}=\frac{c}{\theta}$, which gives also the profit maximizing price as a function of unit costs.

5. The capital market no-arbitrage condition: Deriving equation (9)

In a more general notation the intertemporal zero-profit condition (7) can be expressed as $y(t)=\int_t^\infty \exp\left[-(R(\tau)-R(t))\right]x(\tau)d\tau$ with $R(u)=\int_0^u r(s)ds$. Deriving this function with respect to time yields

$$\dot{y}(t)=-x(t)+\int_t^\infty \frac{\partial}{\partial t}\left(\exp\left[-(R(\tau)-R(t))\right]x(\tau)\right)d\tau$$

$$=-x(t)+\int_t^\infty \dot{R}(t)\exp\left[-(R(\tau)-R(t))\right]x(\tau)d\tau=-x(t)+\dot{R}(t)y(t).$$

With $\dot{R}(t)=\frac{\partial}{\partial t}\int_0^t r(s)ds=r(t)$ the derivative of the intertemporal zero-profit condition with respect to time is $\dot{y}(t)=-x(t)+r(t)y(t)$. With $y(t)=\phi$, $\dot{\phi}=0$ and $x(t)=\pi^i$ we obtain equation (9).

*Chapter 3: Unequal factor prices and incomplete specialization in a Heckscher-Ohlin model of endogenous growth**

1. Introduction

It is a central result of the pure theory of international trade based on two-factors, two-goods Heckscher-Ohlin models that – under certain conditions – trade leads to factor-price equalization (FPE) if countries are incompletely specialized. Factor rewards will usually not equalize if at least one country is completely specialized. Necessary assumptions for FPE in the case of incomplete specialization are free trade, absence of transportation costs, both countries producing with the same technology and the absence of factor-intensity reversals, but, as is well-known, no international mobility of factors is required. This dichotomy of free trade can be found, additionally to text book treatments of the simple two-country, two-homogeneous-goods case (e.g. Gandolfo, 1986, p. I 77) in static models of inter- and intra-industrial trade (Helpman and Krugman, 1985, ch. 7) as well as in dynamic models of innovation and growth (Grossman and Helpman, 1991a, ch. 7.1). Unequal factor rewards, however, are not automatically linked to complete specialization. A situation of incomplete specialization of both countries and no equalization of factor prices can occur, too, with all the conditions mentioned above being satisfied. In order to demonstrate this effect we will build on the model of Grossman and Helpman (1991a, ch. 7.1) who derived the properties of the balanced growth path[1] under the assumption of identical interest rates in both countries, due to either free international mobility of financial capital or identical discount factors of the representative consumer in both countries. That's why they can suggest that "factor price equalization obtains as a long-run proposition in any steady state in which both countries are incompletely specialized" (Grossman and Helpman, 1991a, p. 183).

---

* This chapter follows closely Wälde (1994b).

1 We define a balanced growth path as a solution of a dynamic model where some variables grow at a constant rate (Grossman and Helpman call such a solution a steady state).

In what follows we assume exogenously given fixed discount rates (time preference rates) differing from one country to the other which leads to a balanced growth path being characterized by an absence of FPE, though both countries remain incompletely specialized. In order to make the presentation self-contained we will present the model in the next section where the countries are assumed to be identical in any respect, apart from discount rates. The assumption of differing discount rates implies different interest rates in both countries, which excludes, if we allow for internationally mobile capital (as we will do in the fourth section), a balanced growth path. Thus in the third section we make the usual Heckscher-Ohlin model assumption of internationally immobile physical and financial capital and study the consequences of differing individual discount rates for firm size, trade patterns and notably factor rewards. The effects of different interest rates due to different discount rates were already investigated by Stiglitz (1970) in a Heckscher-Ohlin growth model. In his model at least one country had to specialize: Different interest rates imply different prices which would be a contradiction to the assumption of free trade in *homogeneous* goods. Here this does not present a problem, and, as a matter of fact, is at the center of explanation, since the model includes one differentiated good. In the fourth section we show that internationally mobile financial capital leads to an equalization of factor prices. Finally some conclusions are drawn.

2. A two-country world

Consumption side

Assuming a bequest motive for all households, we let consumers of country i $(i = A, B)$ maximize their discounted stream of future utility with an infinite time horizon. The utility function reads

$$U^i(t) = \int_t^{\infty} \exp\left[-\rho^i(\tau - t)\right] u^i(\tau) d\tau, \qquad 0 < \theta, \sigma < 1, \tag{1}$$

where $u^i(\tau) = \log\left[\left(\int_0^n (x^j)^\theta dj\right)^{\sigma/\theta} Z^{1-\sigma}\right]$ is instantaneous utility resulting from the consumption of a differentiated good X and a homogeneous good Z. The time preference rate is denoted by ρ^i and $n = n^A + n^B$ stands for the number of varieties available for consumption. Given the "felicity" function $u^i(\tau)$, a fraction σ of households' current expenditure E^i will be spent for the differentiated high-tech good and the remaining fraction 1-σ for the homogeneous good (say, food). With these static optimality conditions inserted into the utility function (1), we can maximize it with respect to current expenditure subject to an intertemporal budget constraint of the form

$$E^i(t)+\dot{A}^i(t)=r^i(t)A^i(t)+w_L^i(t)L+w_H^i(t)H, \tag{2}$$

to derive an optimal allocation of expenditure over time. The flow budget constraint (2), expressed for economy i as a whole, equates current expenditure plus the change of asset holdings (a dot indicates the derivative with respect to time) to income from assets, $r^i(t)A^i(t)$, labour, $w_L^i(t)L$, and human capital, $w_H^i(t)H$. As can be seen from (2), households in country i own assets of value $A^i(t)$, L units of labour, and H units of human capital.

The maximization procedure gives demand of country i for variety k of the form (cf. appendix, chapter 2)

$$x^k=\frac{\left(p_x^k\right)^{-\varepsilon}\sigma}{\int_0^{n^A}\left(p_x^j\right)^{1-\varepsilon}dj+\int_{n^A}^{n^A+n^B}\left(p_x^j\right)^{1-\varepsilon}dj}E^i,\quad k\in\left[0,n^A+n^B\right], \tag{3}$$

where p_x^k is the price of variety k and $\varepsilon=1/(1-\theta)$ is the elasticity of substitution between any two varieties. With p_Z denoting the price for food we can write demand for the homogeneous good as

$$Z^i=\frac{1-\sigma}{p_Z}E^i. \tag{4}$$

Since firms have identical technologies and factor rewards equalize between sectors, all varieties produced in one country are equally priced. Thus the aggregate demand functions for each variety produced in country i yields

$$x^i=\frac{X^i}{n^i}=\frac{\left(p_x^i\right)^{-\varepsilon}}{n^A\left(p_x^A\right)^{1-\varepsilon}+n^B\left(p_x^B\right)^{1-\varepsilon}}\sigma\left(E^A+E^B\right),\quad i=A,B. \tag{5}$$

The optimal intertemporal allocation of expenditure is a function of the difference of the current interest rate r^i and the discount rate ρ^i (cf. appendix)

$$\frac{\dot{E}^i}{E^i} = r^i - \rho^i. \tag{6}$$

Production side

The production side of the economies is characterized by three activities all using human capital and labour as input: R&D and manufacturing of one homogeneous and one differentiated final good. The R&D sector is the most human capital intensive one followed by the high-tech manufacturing sector: $h_R^i > h_X^i > h_Z^i$ where h_j^i, $j = R, X, Z$ is the human capital intensity of sector *j* in country *i*.

The production process in the perfectly competitive food industry follows well-behaved linear homogeneous production functions. Therefore, under free trade, the price of each output must equal its unit costs,

$$p_Z = c_Z\left(w_L^A, w_H^A\right) = c_Z\left(w_L^B, w_H^B\right), \tag{7}$$

where $c_Z\left(w_L^i, w_H^i\right)$ is the unit cost function of sector *Z* for both countries depending on factor rewards for labour and human capital. The production sector of the differentiated good is characterized by monopolistic competition. The profit maximizing price set by the manufacturers lies above unit production costs, derived from a production process with constant returns to scale, and equals (cf. appendix, chapter 2)

$$p_x^i = \frac{1}{\theta} c_x\left(w_L^i, w_H^i\right), \tag{8}$$

and thus, profits are

$$\pi^i = \left(p_x^i\right)^{1-\varepsilon} \frac{(1-\theta)\sigma\left(E^A + E^B\right)}{n^A\left(p_x^A\right)^{1-\varepsilon} + n^B\left(p_x^B\right)^{1-\varepsilon}}. \tag{9}$$

In the R&D sector new varieties are produced using human capital, unskilled labour and "knowledge" (*Kn*) as input. As a by-product of the development of new blueprints, non-appropriable knowledge itself is increased (Romer, 1990) which is assumed to be immediately available in both countries as an input for the production of new varieties. Formally, the production function for blueprints is $\dot{n}^i = f_R\left(H_R^i, L_R^i\right)Kn$ with constant returns-to-scale in H and L. Knowledge is assumed to increase proportionally to the measure $n = n^A + n^B$ of the number of varieties. Thus with a suitable choice of units *Kn* can be set equal to *n*. As is well known, it is this technological external effect which leads to positive long-run growth rates.

To conclude the production side, we have to make assumptions about profits in the differentiated good sector. Allowing for free entry and exit, this sector will be producing subject to a zero-profit condition. Since we are in a dynamic framework, it is formulated in the present-value sense and equates discounted future profits to R&D costs $c_R\left(w_L^i, w_H^i\right)/\left(n^A+n^B\right)$[2]. With v^i defined as the present value of a firm by

$$v^i(t)=\int_t^{\infty}\exp\left[-\left(R(\tau)-R(t)\right)\right]\pi^i(\tau)d\tau, \tag{10}$$

where $R(u)=\int_0^u r(s)ds$ is the discount factor depending on the interest rate $r(s)$, the intertemporal zero-profit condition yields

$$v^i=c_R\left(w_L^i, w_H^i\right)/\left(n^A+n^B\right). \tag{11}$$

Differentiating (10) with respect to time yields the usual no-arbitrage conditions for a capital market which expresses the indifference of agents between a riskless loan or buying a share of a firm:

$$\pi^i+\dot{v}^i=r^i v^i. \tag{12}$$

Numeraire and factor-market equilibrium

Since the economy lacks a monetary instrument we can choose (the time path of) one variable as numeraire. Due to the homotheticity of the demand functions (3) and (4) the sum of the individual demand functions is always of the form $f(\cdot)\left(E^A+E^B\right)$ which suggests the normalization of total expenditure $E=E^A+E^B$ to unity. This implies, as will be proven in the third section, that on the balanced growth path, interest rates are given by time preference rates: $r^i=\rho^i$.

Finally we have to specify factor market clearing conditions. The supply of factors is assumed to be totally inelastic, the unit demand functions for factors, a_{ij}, result from cost minimization and the application of Shephard's lemma. With the

2 The expression for R&D unit costs and R&D unit demand functions can be derived from the production function of the R&D sector.

assumption that factor rewards adjust such that markets clear at every moment in time we obtain (cf. appendix)

$$a_{LR}\left(w_L^i, w_H^i\right)\frac{n^i}{n}\frac{\dot{n}^i}{n^i} + a_{LX}\left(w_L^i, w_H^i\right)X^i + a_{LZ}\left(w_L^i, w_H^i\right)Z^i = L,$$
$$a_{HR}\left(w_L^i, w_H^i\right)\frac{n^i}{n}\frac{\dot{n}^i}{n^i} + a_{HX}\left(w_L^i, w_H^i\right)X^i + a_{HZ}\left(w_L^i, w_H^i\right)Z^i = H. \tag{13}$$

With this specification of the model, we can now present the implications of different individual discount rates on a balanced growth path where borrowing and lending between countries is excluded.

Balanced growth path

What we are interested in is under which conditions total output grows in either country in the long run at a constant positive rate and both countries produce both the differentiated good and the homogeneous good. On the balanced growth path nominal and real factor rewards and hence commodity prices are constant[3]. By solving the aggregate demand function (5) for X^i and differentiating it with respect to time we see that this implies that both countries innovate at the same rate: $\dot{n}^A/n^A = \dot{n}^B/n^B$. An intuitive argument for that can be given: If the innovation rates differed, the share of the varieties of one country would approach zero and this country would tend towards a complete specialization in the long run. Then with this implication and from differentiating equation (11) with respect to time we realize that the value of the firm falls at the same rate as the number of varieties (= number of firms) increases: $\dot{n}^A/n^A = -\dot{v}^A/v^A$, $\dot{n}^B/n^B = -\dot{v}^B/v^B$.

By some rearrangements it can easily be shown that with these properties time derivatives are eliminated and the model can be solved for its balanced growth path values[4]: First, solve (12) for $g := -\dot{v}^i/v^i$ and replace v^i by inserting equation (11) which gives

3 The fact that nominal factor rewards are constant is a result of the choice of the numeraire. Real factor rewards, however, are constant independently of which numeraire is chosen.

4 Here we only mention the steps how to obtain a static equation system. The resulting system itself can be found in the appendix.

$$g^i = \frac{\pi^i}{c_R\left(w_L^i, w_H^i\right)/\left(n^A + n^B\right)} - \rho^i, \text{ where } \pi^i = \frac{\left(p_x^i\right)^{1-\varepsilon}(1-\theta)\sigma}{n^A\left(p_x^A\right)^{1-\varepsilon} + n^B\left(p_x^B\right)^{1-\varepsilon}}, \; i = A, B.$$

Second, by using the balanced growth path conditions, replace $\dot{n}^i/n^i = -\dot{v}^i/v^i = g$ in (13) by this expression and find that after these transformations, the model on the balanced growth path can be formulated as consisting of three goods market clearing conditions, given by equation (5) $(i = A, B)$ and by the equation aggregating demand for the homogeneous good to

$$Z^A + Z^B = \frac{1-\sigma}{p_Z},$$

four pricing equations (7) and (8), four factor market clearing conditions (13) and three equations determining the balanced growth path: $g^A = g^B$, $g^A = -\dot{v}^A/v^A$ and $g^B = -\dot{v}^B/v^B$. With these (fourteen) equations wages $w_L^A, w_H^A, w_L^B, w_H^B$, output of the homogeneous and differentiated good Z^A, Z^B, X^A, X^B, growth rates for either country, prices p_x^A, p_x^B, p_Z and the ratio n^A/n^B can be determined.

Cone of diversification

We now have to derive conditions under which the output of both goods in both countries is positive. Since our analysis is a generalization of the Grossman and Helpman (1991a, ch. 7) model since it allows both for identical and different individual discount rates, our conditions can be expected to be similar to those of the original model. In fact, the boundaries of the cone of diversification we derive (cf. appendix) are given by $h_Z^i L^i < H^i < h_{RX}^i L^i$ where h_{RX}^i is the human capital intensity in the composite sector *RX* (consider the R&D sector and the sector producing the differentiated good as one sector) in country *i*. Thus under the (usual) condition that both countries lie within these lines (cf. figure 3.1) we have shown that a balanced growth path with positive output of both goods, positive growth rates[5] and differing individual discount rates exists. We will now turn to the determination of wages and trade patterns.

---

[5] The growth rate is positive if e.g. the time preference rates are sufficiently small.

3. Factor rewards, firm size and trade patterns

Factor rewards and firm size

Usually FPE can be inferred for a certain range of factor endowments. Factor prices are equalized (e.g. Dixit and Norman, 1980; Helpman, 1981; Helpman and Krugman, 1985, ch. 7; Grossman and Helpman, 1991a, ch. 7) as long as factor endowments of the countries are not too dissimilar. Here it is the assumption of different time preference rates which excludes an equalization. We first show that on a balanced growth path with internationally immobile financial capital each country's expenditure is constant.

Proposition 1

On the balanced growth path, the expenditure of each country is constant.

$$E^i(t) = const.$$

Proof: Assets held by consumers in country i amount to (the time index is suppressed) $A^i = n^i v^i$. Thus, the capital market no-arbitrage condition (12) can be written as $r^i A^i = r^i n^i v^i = n^i \pi^i + n^i \dot{v}^i$. Insert this equation into the budget constraint of country i and find $E^i + \dot{A}^i = n^i \pi^i + n^i \dot{v}^i + w_L^i L^i + w_H^i H^i$. Since on the balanced growth path goods prices and factor rewards are constant, $n^i \dot{v}^i = n^i c_R\left(w_L^i, w_H^i\right)\left(-\left(\dot{n}^A + \dot{n}^B\right)/\left(n^A + n^B\right)^2\right) = const.$ by (11) and $\dot{A}^i = 0$, expenditure of country i is constant, too. ◊

Since $E^i(t) = const.$, equation (6) implies that interest rates equal subjective discount rates: $r^i = \rho^i$. Now remember, that on the balanced growth path the value of the representative firm in each country must fall at the same rate. Using (12) and (11) and taking into account that $r^i = \rho^i$, this can be expressed as

$$\rho^A - \left(n^A + n^B\right)\pi^A / c_R\left(w_L^A, w_H^A\right) = \rho^B - \left(n^A + n^B\right)\pi^B / c_R\left(w_L^B, w_H^B\right). \quad (14)$$

This relationship serves to prove the following proposition.

Proposition 2

If on the balanced growth path both countries are incompletely specialized then factor price equalization is excluded as long as individual discount rates differ.

$$\rho^A \neq \rho^B \Rightarrow \neg\left(w_L^A = w_L^B \wedge w_H^A = w_H^B\right).$$

Proof: Insert (9) into (14). Rearranging shows that (cf. appendix) $\operatorname{sgn}\left[\rho^A - \rho^B\right] = \operatorname{sgn}\left[\frac{\left(c_x^A\right)^{1-\varepsilon}}{c_R^A} - \frac{\left(c_x^B\right)^{1-\varepsilon}}{c_R^B}\right]$, where $c_j^i \equiv c_j\left(w_L^i, w_H^i\right)$, $j = X, R$. Now assume that factor prices equalize. Then $c_x^A = c_x^B$ and $c_R^A = c_R^B$ and thus the RHS is zero. This however, contradicts the assumption of different discount factors. Thus factor prices equalization is excluded. ◊

What do unequal factor rewards and incomplete specialization imply in the presence of a differentiated good? Since factor prices differ and the price for the homogeneous good equalizes after the opening up to trade, the price of the differentiated good in country A differs from the one in country B. Consequently the firms are of different size, too, and the firm selling at a lower price will produce more of its variety. This effect of different firm size can be traced back to the difference in discount factors in a direct way by looking at equation (10): Since interest rates equal individual discount rates, profits are discounted by the factor $\exp\left[-\rho^i(\tau - t)\right]$. In static models the zero-profit condition determines the size of the representative firm; if we draw an analogy to dynamic models then it is clear that the firm size must differ as long as the discount factors differ.

Trade patterns

Let us now illustrate our results by figure 3.1. The boundaries of the cone of diversification are marked by the straight lines starting from the origin in the lower left corner (country A) and in the upper right corner (country B). Whereas usually this cone of diversification is a parallelogram, this is not the case here since the slope of the borderlines are given by the factor intensities of sector Z and the composite sector RX which are functions of factor rewards. Since in depicting the figure we assumed that the consumers in country A are more patient than in country B $\left(\rho^A < \rho^B\right)$ and the R&D sector is the most human capital intensive one, the demand for human capital in country A is relatively higher than in country B. By intuition it follows that the ratio of factor rewards in country A is higher than in country B $\left(w_H^A / w_L^A > w_H^B / w_L^B\right)$[6] which implies a lower capital intensity in country A than in country B $\left(h_j^A < h_j^B,\ j = R, X, Z\right)$[7].

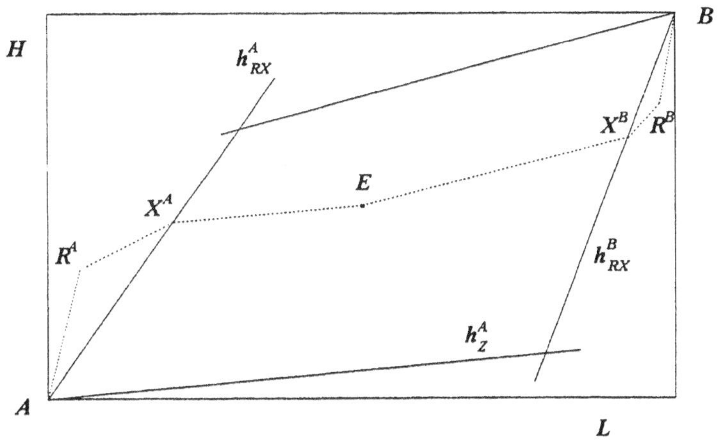

Figure 3.1: The allocation of factors for two countries which differ only in the subjective discount rate

The figure further shows the separate resource endowments of the two countries by point E which was chosen to lie on the intersection point of the diagonals of the rectangle in order to exclude all influence of factor endowments on trade patterns. In models with factor price equalization this would imply that neither country would export the homogeneous good and only intra-industrial trade of the

6 An exact proof of this conjecture would require to totally differentiate a system consisting of fourteen equations (cf. appendix, The static equation system). The expected insights do not seem rewarding enough since the result is of no importance for the main conclusion about trade patterns: In any cases inter- as well as intra-industrial trade will be observed, though countries are of identical size. Chapter 4 derives the relationship between trade patterns and time preference rates in a more rigorous way.

7 In depicting figure 1 we suppose that $h_j^A < h_j^B,\ j = R, X, Z$ implies $h_{RX}^A < h_{RX}^B$.

differentiated good could be observed. The factor allocation in our case can be constructed in the usual way: Draw a parallel starting from E to the h_Z^A-line and connect the intersection point X^A and the origin A by two lines with a slope of h_R^A and h_X^A. With an identical procedure the partition of factors between sectors can be unambiguously determined for country B. Due to different human capital intensities, country A will import the labour intensive good and *net*-export the differentiated high-tech good: The lower h_Z^A and h_{RX}^A the more country A specializes in the production of good X, which holds equivalently for country B. Thus, though both countries are of identical size, there is (standard) intra-industrial as well as inter-industrial trade[8].

4. International mobility of capital

In the last section we have seen that internationally immobile financial capital leads to interest rates which differ between countries. Capital which is perfectly mobile will move to the country where its reward is higher until interest rates are equalized. Therefore on a balanced growth path with internationally mobile capital the evolution of expenditure of country i is given by $\dot{E}^i/E^i = r - \rho^i$ where r is the world interest rate. World expenditure is still normalized at unity which implies that the increase of the expenditure of country A equals the decrease of expenditure of country B: $\dot{E}^A = -\dot{E}^B$. Inserting equation (6) we obtain in addition to $E^A + E^B = 1$ a second equation for E^A and E^B which reads

$$\left(r-\rho^A\right)E^A = -\left(r-\rho^B\right)E^B. \tag{15}$$

This allows to give an explicit expression for the countries' expenditures which read $E^A = \left(\rho^B - r\right)/\left(\rho^B - \rho^A\right)$ and $E^B = \left(r-\rho^A\right)/\left(\rho^B-\rho^A\right)$. Now let countries trade in assets. The interest rate which results must lie between the boundaries given by the time preference rates, $\rho^A < r < \rho^B$, since otherwise both countries would either increase or decrease their expenditures which is a contradiction to $E^A + E^B = 1$. Then, as time goes by (cf. equation (6)), the expenditure of country A rises whereas the expenditure of country B falls which means by equation (15) that the world interest rate approaches ρ^A. This accelerates the decrease of E^B and

[8] See Shimomura (1993) who studies the relation between time preference rates and trade patterns in the presence of durable consumption goods.

slows down the increase of E^A until in the long run (strictly speaking as a limit) the expenditure of the low-time-preference country will equal unity and the expenditure of the high-time preference country will be zero. This is the result as described by Blanchard and Fischer (1989, p.70) for a closed economy with heterogeneous consumers which differ in their time preference rate. The consumer with the lowest time preference rate will eventually own all capital whereas all other consumers' share in total consumption approaches zero. In our economy this implies that country B will export all of its production which will be consumed in country A and transfers its export income to country A.

Of course this is an extreme prediction of income distribution, which is mentioned here only for the fact that with international mobility of capital, factor prices will be equalized[9]: Since interest rates are equal, equation (14) implies
$c_x(w_L^A, w_H^A)/c_R(w_L^A, w_H^A) = c_x(w_L^B, w_H^B)/c_R(w_L^B, w_H^B)$.
This equation, together with $c_Z(w_L^A, w_H^A) = c_Z(w_L^B, w_H^B)$ (derived from equation (7)), can be satisfied only if factor prices are equalized, since both $c_x(\cdot)/c_R(\cdot)$ and $c_Z(\cdot)$ are monotonic functions.

5. Conclusion

In a two-country Heckscher-Ohlin model of endogenous growth we have shown that a balanced growth path exists where both countries are incompletely specialized and yet factor prices do not equalize. This is due to the assumption of different individual discount rates and possible since one of the two goods is a differentiated product. Since it is produced under monopolistic competition, free trade does not require an equalization of goods prices. In the case of two homogeneous goods, free trade must lead to an equalization of prices, which, due to the one-to-one mapping between goods prices and factor prices (given, inter alia, by the assumption of no factor-intensity reversal), implies equal factor rewards. With one differentiated good, however, prices do not have to be equalized under free trade, since each producer can set her profit-maximizing price. With different prices for the differentiated good the quantity of the cheaper good

9 Compare the paper of Buiter (1981) who derives a similar result.

produced per variety is higher than the quantity for the more expensive good (cf. demand function for x^i). Thus intra-industrial trade no longer implies necessarily identical plant size and consequently factor prices do not equalize.

Though we specified the model for two countries which are of identical size, the absence of FPE holds for any factor endowment which allows for an incomplete specialization of both countries; it does not depend on impediments to trade of any sort, differences in technology or factor-intensity reversal. Consequently, in order that FPE results from free trade in intertemporal Heckscher-Ohlin models another condition has to be satisfied: The equalization of individual discount rates.

Appendix

1. Infinite horizon maximization I

In this section the solution for a general infinite horizon maximization problem is given. Apart from costate variables which are denoted by μ here, the notation follows Léonard and Long (1992).

The problem is given by

$$\max_{c(t)} V = \int_0^\infty v(s(t), c(t), t)\, dt, \tag{P}$$

subject to

$$\dot{s}(t) = f(s(t), c(t), t), \tag{A.1}$$

$$s(0) = s_0, \tag{A.2}$$

where $s(t) \in R^n$, $c(t) \in R^m$.

A feasible path is a pair $(s(t), c(t))$ which satisfies (A.1) and (A.2). It is assumed that V converges for all feasible paths, otherwise the optimality criterion must be redefined.

Defining the *present-value* Hamiltonian H as
$H(t) = v(s(t), c(t), t) + \mu(t) f(s(t), c(t), t)$,

necessary conditions for an optimal solution $(s^*(t), c^*(t))$ for (P) are

$$\frac{\partial H(t)}{\partial c(t)} = 0, \tag{A.3}$$

$$\dot{\mu}(t) = -\frac{\partial H(t)}{\partial s(t)}, \tag{A.4}$$

$$\dot{s}(t) = \frac{\partial H(t)}{\partial \mu(t)} = f(s(t), c(t), t), \tag{A.5}$$

$$s(0) = s_0. \tag{A.6}$$

It is often more convenient to work with the *current-value* Hamiltonian $\mathcal{H}$, which is related to the *present-value* Hamiltonian by $\mathcal{H}(t) = \exp[\rho t] H(t)$. In this case, costates $\lambda(t)$ have to be transformed according to $\lambda(t) = \exp[\rho t]\mu(t)$ (cf. Feichtinger and Hartl, 1986, p. 20). The optimality conditions (applied in chapter 6) are then given by (A.5), (A.6) and

$$\frac{\partial \mathcal{H}(t)}{\partial c(t)} = 0, \tag{A.3'}$$

$$\dot{\lambda}(t) = \rho\lambda - \frac{\partial \mathcal{H}(t)}{\partial s(t)}. \tag{A.4'}$$

The first *m* equations (A.3) ($c(t) \in R^m$) solve the control variables *c*(*t*) as a function of state and costate variables, *s*(*t*) and $\mu(t)$. The next *2n* equations (A.4) and (A.5) ($s(t) \in R^n$) constitute a *2n* dimensional differential equation system. In order to solve it, one needs, in addition to the *n* initial conditions given exogenously for the state variables by (A.2), *n* further conditions for the costate variables.

In the literature and in textbooks on optimal control theory (e.g. Chiang, 1992; Léonard and Long, 1992; Feichtinger and Hartl, 1986), these conditions are usually provided in the form of transversality conditions (TVC) which read

$$\lim_{t\to\infty} \mu^*(t)[s(t) - s^*(t)] \geq 0. \tag{TVC}$$

The Mangasarian condition states that if the Hamiltonian is concave in $(s(t), c(t))$ (cf. Mangasarian, 1966 or Léonard and Long, 1992, p. 288), or, according to the weaker Arrow condition, if the Hamiltonian with all controls *c*(*t*) being substituted out by using (A.3), is concave in states $s(t)$ (cf. Arrow, 1968; Arrow and Kurz, 1970 or Chiang, 1992, p. 217, p. 252), then the TVC is *sufficient* for the optimality of a solution $\left(s^*(t), c^*(t)\right)$. Thus the n conditions to choose the optimal path of costates are provided by n transversality conditions.

The TVC, under certain circumstances, is equivalent to (cf. Léonard and Long, 1992, p. 289)

$$\lim_{t\to\infty} \mu^*(t) s^*(t) = 0. \qquad \text{(TVC')}$$

In the endogenous growth theory literature, (TVC') is considered as a *necessary* condition. An example is Romer (1986, p. 1021) or Rebelo (1988, p.35, footnote 1).

Grossman and Helpman (1991a, p. 34, p. 69) use (TVC'), too, citing Arrow and Kurz (1970) but without mentioning, whether it is necessary or sufficient or both.

The statements that (TVC') is necessary are based on Araujo and Scheinkman (1983). In the following, (TVC') will also be regarded as both sufficient and necessary.

2. Infinite horizon maximization II: Deriving equation (6)

In contrast to chapter 2, the utility function here is maximized subject to a flow budget constraint. Again, as described in the appendix to chapter 2, we will first derive the indirect dynamic utility function and then maximize it, here, subject to a flow budget constraint. The problem reads

$$\max_{E(\tau)} \int_t^\infty \exp\left[-\rho(\tau - t)\right]\left(\ln E^i(\tau) + \ln P^i(\tau)\right) d\tau,$$

subject to

$$E^i(t) + \dot{A}^i(t) = r^i(t) A^i(t) + w_L^i(t) + w_H^i(t) H^i(t). \qquad \text{(A.7)}$$

The current-value Hamiltonian is

$$\mathcal{H}(\tau) = \ln E^i(\tau) + \ln P^i(\tau) + \eta\left(r^i(t) A^i(t) + w_L^i(t) + w_H^i(t) H^i(t) - E^i(t)\right).$$

Necessary and sufficient conditions are (with time index t suppressed) (A.7), initial conditions for A^i and

$$\mathcal{H}_{E^i} = \frac{1}{E^i} - \eta = 0,$$

$$\dot{\eta} = \rho\eta - \eta r,$$

$$\lim_{\tau\to\infty} \exp\left[-\rho(\tau - t)\right] \eta A = 0.$$

Combining the first two first-order conditions, one obtains (6).

3. Deriving equation (13)

Here we derive unit demand functions for the R&D sector. The production function is given (cf. main text) by $\dot{n}^i = f_R(H_R^i, L_R^i)Kn$, where $\dot{n}^i$ indicates how many new blueprints are developed per time unit. By minimizing costs subject to an output constraint $\dot{n}^i = 1$ one can derive unit cost functions for the R&D sector which are given by $c_R(w_L^i, w_H^i)/(n^A + n^B)$. By applying Shephard's lemma, we obtain unit demand functions for factor f, where w_f is the factor reward of that factor:

$$\frac{\partial}{\partial w_f}\frac{c_R(w_L^i, w_H^i)}{n^A + n^B} = \frac{\partial}{\partial w_f} c_R(w_L^i, w_H^i)\frac{1}{n} := a_{fR}(w_L^i, w_H^i)\frac{1}{n}.$$

Multiplying by the output of this sector gives

$$a_{fR}(w_L^i, w_H^i)\frac{1}{n}\dot{n}^i = a_{fR}(w_L^i, w_H^i)\frac{n^i}{n}\frac{\dot{n}^i}{n^i}$$

4. The static equation system

Solving (12) for $g := -\dot{v}^i/v^i$ and replacing v^i by inserting equation (11) gives

$$g^i = \frac{\pi^i}{c_R(w_L^i, w_H^i)/(n^A + n^B)} - \rho^i, \text{ where } \pi^i = \frac{(p_x^i)^{1-\varepsilon}(1-\theta)\sigma}{n^A(p_x^A)^{1-\varepsilon} + n^B(p_x^B)^{1-\varepsilon}}.$$

These two equations ($i = A, B$) in addition to $g^A = g^B \equiv g$ are the balanced growth path conditions. The four factor market clearing conditions then read

$$a_{LR}(w_L^i, w_H^i)\frac{n^i}{n}g + a_{LX}(w_L^i, w_H^i)X^i + a_{LZ}(w_L^i, w_H^i)Z^i = L,$$

$$a_{HR}(w_L^i, w_H^i)\frac{n^i}{n}g + a_{HX}(w_L^i, w_H^i)X^i + a_{HZ}(w_L^i, w_H^i)Z^i = H.$$

The goods markets equilibrium conditions are

$$X^i = \frac{n^i(p_x^i)^{-\varepsilon}\sigma}{n^A(p_x^A)^{1-\varepsilon} + n^B(p_x^B)^{1-\varepsilon}}, \qquad Z^A + Z^B = \frac{1-\sigma}{p_Z}.$$

The pricing equations are

$$p_Z = c_Z(w_L^A, w_H^A) = c_Z(w_L^B, w_H^B), \qquad p_x^i = \frac{1}{\theta}c_x(w_L^i, w_H^i).$$

These fourteen equations allow to determine equilibrium values for wages $w_L^A, w_H^A, w_L^B, w_H^B$, output of the homogeneous and differentiated good Z^A, Z^B, X^A, X^B, growth rates for either country, prices p_x^A, p_x^B, p_Z and the ratio n^A/n^B.

5. Cone of diversification

The idea underlying the derivation of the condition $h_Z^i L^i < H^i < h_{RX}^i L^i$ for positive output of X and Z is the following: First treat (for each country) the R&D sector and the manufacturing sector X as a composite sector RX (both activities are undertaken by the same firms) and derive conditions under which positive quantities of factors are allocated both to sector RX and to sector Z. Then show that if positive quantities of factors are allocated to sector RX, these factors are further subdivided (in positive quantities) between R&D and manufacturing in X. If this holds the country produces both goods and undertakes R&D, i.e. it is incompletely specialized.

We first show that positive quantities of factors are allocated both to the composite sector RX and to sector Z if (the country index is suppressed in the sequel) $h_Z L < H < h_{RX} L$:

We can write the factor market clearing conditions as

$$(L_R + L_X) + L_Z = L,$$

$$h_{RX}(L_R + L_X) + h_Z L_Z = H.$$

where $h_{RX} = (H_R + H_X)/(L_R + L_X)$ is the human capital intensity of the composite sector RX and $h_Z = H_Z/L_Z$ is the human capital intensity of sector Z. Solving for $(L_R + L_X)$ and L_Z yields the above condition $h_Z L < H < h_{RX} L$ for $(L_R + L_X)$ and L_Z to be positive.

Now we show that if $L_R + L_X$ is positive then a (positive) subdivision of factors between R&D and the manufacturing sector follows from our assumption of human capital intensities $h_R > h_X > h_Z$:

Rewrite the factor market clearing conditions as

$$L_R + L_X = L - L_Z, \qquad h_R L_R + h_X L_X = H - H_Z.$$

Solving this system for L_R and L_X shows that both are positive if $h_X < (H_R + H_X)/(L_R + L_X)$. This is always fulfilled under our (standard) assumption $h_R > h_X > h_Z$. (The proof is analogous to the proofs of section 6. Lemmas, below.) ◊

6. Proof of the proposition 2

Proposition

$$\rho^A \neq \rho^B \Rightarrow \neg\left(w_L^A = w_L^B \wedge w_H^A = w_H^B\right).$$

Proof:

We know that on the balanced growth path

$\rho^A - \left(n^A + n^B\right)\pi^A / c_R\left(w_L^A, w_H^A\right) = \rho^B - \left(n^A + n^B\right)\pi^B / c_R\left(w_L^B, w_H^B\right).$

This equation can be, after inserting profit and pricing equations, rewritten with $c_j^i \equiv c_j\left(w_L^i, w_H^i\right)$, $j = X, R$ as

$$\rho^A - \frac{(1-\theta)\sigma\left(c_x^A\right)^{1-\varepsilon}}{\left(n^A\left(c_x^A\right)^{1-\varepsilon} + n^B\left(c_x^B\right)^{1-\varepsilon}\right)c_R^A}\left(n^A + n^B\right) = \rho^B - \frac{(1-\theta)\sigma\left(c_x^B\right)^{1-\varepsilon}}{\left(n^A\left(c_x^A\right)^{1-\varepsilon} + n^B\left(c_x^B\right)^{1-\varepsilon}\right)c_R^B}\left(n^A + n^B\right).$$

Rearranging yields

$$\rho^A - \rho^B = \frac{(1-\theta)\sigma\left(n^A + n^B\right)}{n^A\left(c_x^A\right)^{1-\varepsilon} + n^B\left(c_x^B\right)^{1-\varepsilon}}\left(\frac{\left(c_x^A\right)^{1-\varepsilon}}{c_R^A} - \frac{\left(c_x^B\right)^{1-\varepsilon}}{c_R^B}\right).$$

From this condition it is immediately clear that if $\rho^A \neq \rho^B$ then $\dfrac{\left(c_x^A\right)^{1-\varepsilon}}{c_R^A} \neq \dfrac{\left(c_x^B\right)^{1-\varepsilon}}{c_R^B}$.

Assume that factor prices equalize. Then $c_x^A = c_x^B$ and $c_R^A = c_R^B$ and thus the RHS is zero. This however, contradicts the assumption of different discount factors. Thus factor prices equalization is excluded. ◊

7. Lemmas

These lemmas show that the limiting lines of the cone of diversification must lie below and above the diagonal of the rectangle such that a cone of diversification can exist.

Lemma 1

If the factor intensities h_i for sectors $i = R, X, Z$ can be uniquely ranked such that $h_R > h_X > h_Z$ then $h_Z < \frac{H}{L}$, given incomplete specialization.

Proof

The factor intensities are defined as $h_i := \frac{H_i}{L_i}, i = R, X, Z$. By assumption $h_R > h_X > h_Z$. Thus $h_Z L_R < H_R, h_Z L_X < H_X$ and $h_Z L_Z = H_Z$. Summing up these three equations yields $h_Z(L_R + L_X + L_Z) < H_R + H_X + H_Z$ and we find

$$\frac{H}{L} = \frac{H_R + H_X + H_Z}{L_R + L_X + L_Z} > \frac{h_Z(L_R + L_X + L_Z)}{L_R + L_X + L_Z} = h_Z. \qquad \Diamond$$

Lemma 2

If the factor intensities h_i for sectors $i = R, X, Z$ can be uniquely ranked such that $h_R > h_X > h_Z$ then $h_{RX} := \frac{H_R + H_X}{L_R + L_X} > \frac{H}{L}$, given incomplete specialization.

Proof

The factor intensities are defined as $h_i := \frac{H_i}{L_i}, i = R, X, Z$. By assumption $h_R > h_X > h_Z$. Thus $h_X L_R < H_R$. Consequently

$h_Z < h_X = h_X \frac{L_R + L_X}{L_R + L_X} = \frac{h_X L_R + H_X}{L_R + L_X} < \frac{H_R + H_X}{L_R + L_X} = h_{RX}$. With $h_Z < h_{RX}$ results $H_Z < h_{RX} L_Z$. This finally gives

$$h = \frac{H_R + H_X + H_Z}{L_R + L_X + L_Z} < \frac{h_{RX}(L_R + L_X) + h_{RX} L_Z}{L_R + L_X + L_Z} = h_{RX}. \qquad \Diamond$$

Chapter 4: Transitional dynamics, convergence and international capital flows in two-country models of innovation and growth

1. Introduction

In the last chapter we restricted our attention to the balanced growth path, a standard approach for many models of endogenous growth. In this chapter the stability properties of a related balanced growth path are studied[1]. Nearly the entire literature of the "new" growth theory bases its results on an analysis of the balanced growth path (BGP). Such an analysis, however, has to be extended by a study of the stability properties of the BGP since *a priori* it is not clear whether trajectories leading to a BGP exist for all possible, historically given initial conditions. Mulligan (1991) and Mulligan and Sala-i-Martin (1993) describe a general approach, how transitional dynamics can be analyzed. Mulligan and Sala-i-Martin (1993) apply this method to a class of models characterized by the accumulation of two factors of production. The models analyzed include e.g. the Lucas (1988) model which is shown to be, at least for some parameter values, saddle path stable. This means that independently of initial conditions, all variables converge monotonically to their BGP trajectories and that a study of the properties of the BGP is a good proxy for describing the general behaviour of the model economy. In contrast to this results, Benhabib and Perli (1993) emphasise, that the BGP of the Lucas (1988) model is not necessarily saddle path stable, but can rather be reached, for certain parameter values, by a continuum of paths. If this is the case, BGP analysis is too narrow to derive statements about the behaviour of the model.

The stability properties of the Rivera-Batiz and Romer (1991) model on economic integration and endogenous growth is studied by Devereux and Lapham (1993). Since the model they analyze is characterized by technological spillovers which are

---

1 Studying the stability properties of the balanced growth path of the last chapter would lead to huge technical complications without yielding further insight. Thus we undertake our analysis in a model with only one factor of production and where time preference rates of consumers in country A and country B do not differ.

restricted to the national economies they find that the BGP is unstable. This result recalls the model by Grossman and Helpman (1991a, ch. 8) on hysteresis in trade, where the instability of the BGP with innovation of new goods taking place in both economies is shown to be due to the restricted flow of knowledge. A similar method as the one presented by Mulligan and Sala-i-Martin was used by Faig (1991).

In this chapter we study transitional dynamics in a typical two-country model of innovation and growth, which is based on the model by Grossman and Helpman (1991a, ch. 3.2). It is to be understood as a prototype which gives general ideas about the stability properties of more complex models of that kind. There are at least two reasons, why transitional dynamics are important in this setting: First, an economy can be pushed off its BGP by any small shock to its R&D activities and, second, extremely important in an international trade setting, two countries which trade with each other will certainly not find themselves on a BGP immediately after opening up to trade but will rather have to go through a period of adjustment. The usual approach compares, in static models, two points in time (autarky and trade equilibrium) but neglects the period in between, and, in growth models, two disconnected periods in time (autarky and trade BGP). The approach here thus fills the gap of the usual analysis by considering explicitly the behaviour of variables at every point in time from autarky to a long-run trade equilibrium.

The next section presents a two-country model with a positive long-run innovation rate due to a public stock of knowledge. The third section studies the local stability properties of the BGP which are important in the presence of small shocks to the R&D processes and investigates the convergence process near the equilibrium more in detail. The fourth section highlights global stability properties and shows how two initially very unequal economies converge to a common BGP. The fifth section derives the implications for international financial capital flows. Finally, some conclusions are drawn.

2. A typical two-country world of innovation and growth

The model consists of two countries producing one differentiated final good using homogeneous internationally immobile labour as input. Countries interact by trading final goods and financial capital which will give rise to intra-industrial trade and interest rate equalization. We first characterize the behaviour of a representative, infinitely living household and then describe the behaviour of firms in a monopolistic competition setting. Market equilibria conclude the description of the model[2].

Consumption side

Utility of consumers in country i stems from a stream of future "felicities", discounted at the internationally identical time preference rate ρ, given by

$$U^i(t) = \int_t^{\infty} \exp[-\rho(\tau - t)] u^i(\tau) d\tau, \tag{1}$$

where "felicity" $u^i(\tau)$ depends on consumption of varieties k of a differentiated final good x produced in both countries. Letting n^i indicate the (measure of the) number of varieties currently produced in country i $(i = A, B)$, instantaneous utility amounts to

$$u^i(\tau) = \log\left(\int_0^{n^A + n^B} \left(x^k\right)^{\theta} dk\right)^{1/\theta}, \qquad 0 < \theta < 1.$$

It is well known (cf. appendix 1) that these preferences imply that demand of all consumers in country i for a variety k is a function of prices p^k, of the number of differentiated goods and of current expenditure E^i,

$$x^k = \left(p^k\right)^{-\varepsilon} E^i \left(\int_0^{n^A + n^B} \left(p^{k'}\right)^{1-\varepsilon} dk'\right)^{-1}. \qquad k \in \left[0, n^A + n^B\right]$$

The elasticity of substitution between any two varieties is given by $\varepsilon = 1/(1-\theta)$. This demand function is reinserted into (1) which is then maximized with respect to E^i subject to the flow budget constraint

$$E^i(t) + \dot{A}^i(t) = r(t) A^i(t) + w^i(t) L^i, \tag{2}$$

which equates current expenditure and changes of the value of asset holdings $\dot{A}^i(t)$ to asset and labour income, $r(t)A^i(t)$ and $w^i(t)L^i$, respectively, where L^i is the fixed labour endowment of economy i. Since financial capital is assumed to be completely mobile, interest rates $r(t)$ do not differ between countries.

The optimality conditions entail and imply, respectively, an equation determining the optimal allocation of expenditure over time

---

2 Cf. Grossman and Helpman (1991a, ch. 3) for a more detailed discussion of a closed economy version of this model.

$$\frac{\dot{E}^i(t)}{E^i(t)} = r(t) - \rho, \tag{3}$$

the budget constraint for each country as given in (2), two transversality conditions which read

$$\lim_{\tau \to \infty} \exp[-\rho\,\tau] \frac{A^i(\tau)}{E^i(\tau)} = 0, \tag{4}$$

and aggregate world demand for a variety produced in country i, given by

$$x^i = \frac{\left(p^i\right)^{-\varepsilon}}{n^A\left(p^A\right)^{1-\varepsilon} + n^B\left(p^B\right)^{1-\varepsilon}}\left(E^A + E^B\right), \tag{5}$$

where the fact has been used that, as will turn out when looking at the production side, all varieties in country i are equally priced.

Production side

The production side is characterized by two activities: Production of varieties for which blueprints have already been developed and development of new blueprints. The production process takes place under constant returns to scale and follows the simplest possible production function: $x^k = L_x^k$, where L_x^k stands for the quantity of labour allocated to the production of variety k. Since varieties are imperfect substitutes, each producer has some monopoly power and maximizes profits by charging a price (cf. appendix, chapter 2)

$$p^i = w^i / \theta. \tag{6}$$

It is this equation which implies that all varieties produced in country i are equally priced. If the outcome of the model implies factor price equalization, then all goods in the world economy have the same price.

The development of a new blueprint requires the allocation of a certain quantity of labour and some knowledge which is regarded as a public good (Romer, 1990). The production function reads $\dot{n}^i = L_R^i (Kn)^i$, where $(Kn)^i$ represents the knowledge stock available for firms in country i and L_R^i is the quantity of labour of country i, which is allocated to R&D. Knowledge is assumed to be proportional to the number of differentiated goods available in the world economy and thus regarded to flow freely between countries. By a suitable choice of units, this relationship can be expressed by $(Kn)^i = n = n^A + n^B$.

In analogy to static models free entry requires the absence of pure profits. Thus the present value v of the future profit stream resulting from the development of a new blueprint (and the subsequent production and selling of the variety) must equal its development costs and the free-entry condition yields

$$v^i = c_R^i = w^i / n. \tag{7}$$

In a perfect-foresight equilibrium, the value of the firm is determined by its future profits. We obtain

$$v^i(t) = \int_t^\infty \exp\left[-\left(R(\tau) - R(t)\right)\right]\pi^i(\tau)d\tau, \tag{8}$$

where profits $\pi^i(\tau) = \dfrac{(1-\theta)(p^i)^{1-\varepsilon}(E^A + E^B)}{n^A(p^A)^{1-\varepsilon} + n^B(p^B)^{1-\varepsilon}}$ are discounted by a cumulative factor $R(u) = \int_0^u r(s)ds$ depending on the interest rate $r(s)$. Given this value of the firms, the value of assets in the world economy amounts to

$$A = A^A + A^B = n^A v^A + n^B v^B \tag{9}$$

Finally, the full employment condition for the factor market requires that demand for labour of the R&D sector and of the production process equals fixed supply,

$$L_R^i + n^i L_x^k = (\dot{n}^i / n) + n^i x^i = L^i. \tag{10}$$

3. Local stability of the balanced growth path

In this section we derive the reduced form of the model, compute the solution of the model on the BGP and study local stability properties and convergence issues.

Reduced form of the model

The model can be simplified by solving the factor market clearing condition (10) for $\dot{n}^i / n^i$ and combining with aggregate demand functions (5), where (6) and (7) have been inserted . This gives (cf. appendix), with $E = E^A + E^B$

$$\frac{\dot{n}^i}{n^i} = \frac{n}{n^i} L^i - \frac{\theta(v^i)^{-\varepsilon}}{n^A(v^A)^{1-\varepsilon} + n^B(v^B)^{1-\varepsilon}} E. \tag{11}$$

Differentiating (8) with respect to time, computing profits as

$$\pi^i = (1-\theta)\frac{(v^i)^{1-\varepsilon}}{n^A(v^A)^{1-\varepsilon}+n^B(v^B)^{1-\varepsilon}}E,$$

we find

$$\frac{\dot{v}^i}{v^i} = r-(1-\theta)\frac{(v^i)^{-\varepsilon}}{n^A(v^A)^{1-\varepsilon}+n^B(v^B)^{1-\varepsilon}}E. \tag{12}$$

Of course, Walras' Law must hold in this model[3]. Thus we can choose (the timepath of) one price as numeraire and choose it such that total expenditure $E = E^A + E^B$ equals unity. This implies, due to the assumption of internationally completely mobile financial capital, that interest rates are given by the time preference rate at every moment in time (cf. appendix),

$$r = \rho. \tag{13}$$

With this choice of numeraire, the reduced form of the model is[4]

$$\frac{\dot{n}^i}{n^i} = \frac{n}{n^i}L^i - \frac{\theta(v^i)^{-\varepsilon}}{n^A(v^A)^{1-\varepsilon}+n^B(v^B)^{1-\varepsilon}}, \tag{14}$$

$$\frac{\dot{v}^i}{v^i} = \rho-(1-\theta)\frac{(v^i)^{-\varepsilon}}{n^A(v^A)^{1-\varepsilon}+n^B(v^B)^{1-\varepsilon}}. \tag{15}$$

Balanced growth path

On the BGP, both countries innovate at a rate of (cf. appendix) $g = (1-\theta)L - \theta\rho$. This means that new varieties of the differentiated good are developed in both countries at that rate and the value of the representative firm falls at the rate of g. Further, firm values equalize, $v^A = v^B$, and the ratio of number of varieties n^A/n^B is related to endowment by

$$n^A/L^A = n^B/L^B. \tag{16}$$

---

3 The fact that Walras' Law holds can be easily seen by first adding the budget constraint of country A to the budget constraint of country B and then inserting the equilibrium conditions (7), (11) and (12). The equation which results is always fulfilled (cf. appendix).

4 Strictly speaking, the budget constraint of either country should be added to these two equations. Since it is of no importance for stability properties, however, we do not include it here.

The value of all firms V and thus the value of assets A held by consumers amounts to $V = A = n^A v^A + n^B v^B = (n^A + n^B)v = 1/(L+\rho)$ and the value of all firms in country i is $V^i = \frac{1}{L+\rho}\frac{L^i}{L}$.

Eigenvalues of a substitute-model

The initial number of differentiated goods n^A and n^B is given by history which can not be assumed to satisfy the ratio of differentiated goods on the BGP at every moment in time. We will consider here small deviations from the BGP and turn to the question of global stability in the fourth section.

The local stability of the BGP will be analyzed by using a substitute-model which can be deduced from the original model by simple transformations. This approach was introduced into endogenous growth theory by Mulligan (1991) and Mulligan and Sala-i-Martin (1993). The idea consists in transforming the variables of an original model, whose solution is a BGP, in such a way that the solution of the new model is a stationary state (all variables are constant over time). Here, the new variables are defined as

$$x := n^A v^B, \qquad y := n^B v^B, \qquad z := v^A / v^B. \tag{17}$$

It is obvious that with n^A and n^B growing at g and v^A and v^B falling at g, the new variables are constant if the original model is on a BGP. Since one can also conclude from constant new variables to a BGP of the original model, the new system being in a stationary state implies that the original model is on a BGP.

Starting from the reduced form of the original model, given by (14) and (15), we apply the variable transformation and find as the new model (cf. appendix)

$$\begin{aligned}
\dot{x} &= (x+y)L^A + \rho x - \frac{1+\theta(z^{-\varepsilon}-1)}{z^{1-\varepsilon} + yx^{-1}}, \\
\dot{y} &= (x+y)L^B + \rho y - \frac{1}{xy^{-1}z^{1-\varepsilon}+1}, \qquad\qquad x,y,z>0, \\
\dot{z} &= (1-\theta)\frac{z - z^{1-\varepsilon}}{xz^{1-\varepsilon}+y}.
\end{aligned} \tag{S}$$

The local stability of this derived system can be analyzed in a standard way by linearizing around its equilibrium values which are given by (cf. appendix)

$$x^* = \frac{1}{L+\rho}\frac{L^A}{L}, \quad y^* = \frac{1}{L+\rho}\frac{L^B}{L}, \quad z^* = 1. \tag{18}$$

The Jacobian of this system, evaluated at equilibrium values, is (cf. appendix)

$$J = \begin{pmatrix} L^A + \rho - \left(1 + \frac{\rho}{L}\right) L^B & L^A \left(2 + \frac{\rho}{L}\right) & \frac{\theta}{1-\theta} \frac{L^A L^B}{L^2} \\ L^B \left(2 + \frac{\rho}{L}\right) & L^B + \rho - \left(1 + \frac{\rho}{L}\right) L^A & \frac{-\theta}{1-\theta} \frac{L^A L^B}{L^2} \\ 0 & 0 & L + \rho \end{pmatrix}.$$

The eigenvalues λ of J are determined by $|J - \lambda I| = 0$, where I is the identity matrix. Expanding by the last row shows immediately that one eigenvalue is given by $L + \rho$. The other two can be found by solving the remaining quadratic equation. After some rearrangements (cf. appendix), eigenvalues turn out to be $\lambda_{1,2} = L + \rho$ and $\lambda_3 = -L$.

Eigenvalues and stability

Given the eigenvalues of the transformed system, it remains to be discussed what they reveal to us about the stability properties of the original model.

Since we have one eigenvalue with negative real part and two positive ones, the system (S) is locally saddle path stable. This means that one variable can be exogenously given, whereas the other two must be control variables, in order to choose the "right" saddle path. We now have to find out, whether the original model provides enough control variables to ensure that the economy jumps on the stable arm. Assume that x is exogenous, then v^B can be used to choose a correct y and v^A to choose a correct z. Thus, since optimality requires that the transversality conditions (4) are satisfied, consumers will choose initial values indeed such that the economy jumps on the stable saddle path and thus approaches its long-run BGP.

Transitional dynamics and convergence

We now study transitional dynamics near the BGP more in detail. The dynamic behaviour of the two-country world near the BGP is described by the linear differential equation system

$$\left(\dot{\tilde{x}}, \dot{\tilde{y}}, \dot{\tilde{z}}\right)^T = J\left(\tilde{x}, \tilde{y}, \tilde{z}\right)^T, \tag{19}$$

where a tilde denotes the deviations from the stationary state values, $\tilde{\psi} = \psi - \psi^*$, $\psi = x, y, z$; ψ^* are given by (18) and J is the Jacobian given above. A general solution is given by (cf. appendix)

$$\begin{pmatrix} \tilde{x} \\ \tilde{y} \\ \tilde{z} \end{pmatrix} = c_1 \begin{pmatrix} 1 \\ \frac{1}{L^B} \\ \frac{1}{L^A} \\ 0 \end{pmatrix} \exp[(L+\rho)t] + c_2 \begin{pmatrix} 0 \\ \frac{1}{L^A(2+\rho/L)} \\ -\frac{1-\theta}{\theta}\frac{L^2}{L^A L^B} \end{pmatrix} \exp[(L+\rho)t] + c_3 \begin{pmatrix} 1 \\ -1 \\ 0 \end{pmatrix} \exp[-Lt].$$

Taking into consideration that constants c_i are determined by initial conditions, which in turn will be chosen such that the world economy jumps on the stable saddle path leading to a BGP, time paths simplify to

$$\begin{pmatrix} \tilde{x} \\ \tilde{y} \\ \tilde{z} \end{pmatrix} = \tilde{x}_0 \begin{pmatrix} 1 \\ -1 \\ 0 \end{pmatrix} \exp[-Lt].$$

Relating further initial conditions for the transformed variable $\tilde{x}_0$ to initial conditions of the original model by (17), the trajectories on the linearized saddle path are (cf. appendix)

$$\begin{pmatrix} \tilde{x} \\ \tilde{y} \\ \tilde{z} \end{pmatrix} = \frac{1}{L+\rho}\left(\frac{n_0^A}{n_0^B + n_0^A} - \frac{L^A}{L}\right)\begin{pmatrix} 1 \\ -1 \\ 0 \end{pmatrix} \exp[-Lt]. \tag{20}$$

By the definition of $\tilde{\psi}$ in (19) and $z := v^A/v^B$ in (17), the value of firms in both countries are always equalized which is intuitively clear by looking at the definition of the value as the discounted future profit flow in (8): Discount factors and profits of firms in both countries are identical since they depend on values which are the same for all firms in this world economy: Interest rates, the number of competing firms and global expenditure. Note that, as will turn out later, this equality of firm values is not restricted to the linearized saddle path but holds everywhere on the actual, non-linearized, saddle path, too.

Equation (20) further relates initial conditions for historically given quantities of varieties in country A and B to transitional dynamics. If, say, after opening up to trade, initial conditions are such that the expression $\left(n_0^A/\left(n_0^B + n_0^A\right) - L^A/L\right)$ vanishes, no adjustment dynamics will be observed. This makes perfectly sense, since this expression can be readily shown to be satisfied on a BGP by using (16).

Making the opposite conclusion, this implies that the further initial conditions differ from the BGP property (16), the longer convergence and transition towards a suitable defined level close to the BGP will last. For illustration purposes assume a situation where $n^A/L^A > n^B/L^B$. Provided that this is close enough to the BGP, such that (20) approximates dynamics with satisfying accuracy, the ratio of varieties evolves according to (cf. appendix)

$$\frac{n^B}{n^A} = \frac{-\left(\frac{n_0^A}{n_0^B + n_0^A} - \frac{L^A}{L}\right)\exp[-Lt] + \frac{L^B}{L}}{\left(\frac{n_0^A}{n_0^B + n_0^A} - \frac{L^A}{L}\right)\exp[-Lt] + \frac{L^A}{L}}. \tag{21}$$

Since $n^A/L^A > n^B/L^B$ implies $n^A/n > L^A/L$, the ratio n^B/n^A approaches its BGP equilibrium value monotonically from below: $\frac{n^B}{n^A} \xrightarrow{<} \frac{L^B}{L^A}$ starting from $\frac{n_0^B}{n_0^A}$. This is depicted in figure 4.1.

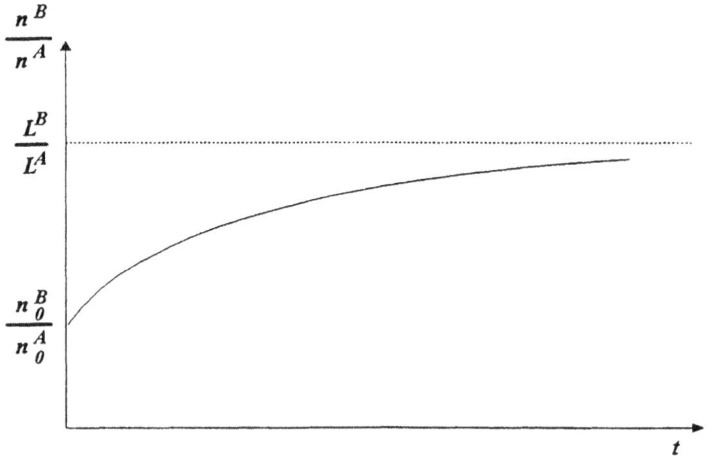

Figure 4.1: Convergence towards the balanced growth path

Thus, in terms of innovation rates, country B will always innovate faster than country A; the difference in innovation rates between countries, however, approaches (but never equals) zero. Strictly speaking, the two-country world will never reach its common BGP.

4. Global stability properties and innovation rates

So far we have restricted our attention to the local behaviour of the system. If situations are studied where two countries begin to trade which are very different in their ratio of differentiated goods to factor endowment, which means that they are far away from their common BGP, then global stability properties become important. In this section we first want to find out whether the system is also globally saddle-path stable and then analyze timepaths of innovation rates during the adjustment period.

Global stability properties

To learn more about global behaviour of the two-country world, we again reduce the dimensionality of the transformed system (S) by one. This is possible by observing that the long-run equilibrium of (S) can be approached only if z jumps immediately to its equilibrium value $z^* = 1$. If the initial value of z is greater than unity, then z would ever grow (independently of the values x and y take) and, analogously, with an initial value smaller than unity, z would ever decrease. Thus in order to be on the stable saddle path, the value of z must, right from the beginning, be unity[5]. Using this fact, system (S) can be written as

$$\begin{aligned} \dot{x} &= (x+y)L^A + \rho x - \frac{x}{x+y}, \\ \dot{y} &= (x+y)L^B + \rho y - \frac{y}{x+y}, \end{aligned} \qquad x, y > 0, \qquad \text{(S')}$$

We now simply have to find the zero-motion loci and can then undertake a phase diagram analysis in the (x,y)-space. The zero-motion loci $(\hat{x}, \hat{y})$ for $\dot{x} = 0$ are given by

$$(\hat{x}+\hat{y})L^A + \rho\hat{x} - \frac{\hat{x}}{\hat{x}+\hat{y}} = 0. \qquad (22)$$

In order to get an idea of where these loci can be found in the positive quadrant (from an economic point of view, only positive values for x and y make sense), we determine the intersection point of these loci with rays starting from the origin,

---

5 This can also be derived from the original model (cf. appendix): By equation (15) $\dot{v}^A/v^A > \dot{v}^B/v^B \Leftrightarrow v^A > v^B$. Since on the BGP $v^A = v^B$, firm values must equalize at every moment in time.

given by $\hat{y} = \alpha\hat{x}$, where α ranges from zero to plus infinity. Inserted into (22), the intersection points are at

$$(1+\alpha)\hat{x}L^A + \rho\hat{x} - (1+\alpha)^{-1} = 0 \Leftrightarrow ((1+\alpha)L^A + \rho)\hat{x} = (1+\alpha)^{-1} \Leftrightarrow \hat{x} = \frac{(1+\alpha)^{-1}}{(1+\alpha)L^A + \rho}.$$

Thus the zero-motion loci are given as a function of α as

$$(\hat{x},\hat{y}) = \left(\frac{(1+\alpha)^{-1}}{(1+\alpha)L^A + \rho}, \alpha\hat{x}\right) = \left(\frac{(1+\alpha)^{-1}}{(1+\alpha)L^A + \rho}, \frac{\alpha(1+\alpha)^{-1}}{(1+\alpha)L^A + \rho}\right).$$

Given this notation, we see that there is one intersection point with the x-axis for $\alpha = 0$ at $\left(\frac{1}{L^A + \rho}, 0\right)$. Letting α increase, $\hat{x}$ decreases and approaches zero as α goes to infinity. $\hat{y}$, however, is not monotonic in α. Since the slope of $\hat{y}$ at $\alpha = 0$ is positive it increases first and then at a certain point must decrease since – apply L'Hôpital's rule – $\hat{y}$ approaches zero as α goes to infinity. Thus we can unambiguously draw the zero-motion loci determined by (22) as in figure 4.2. In an analogous way the zero motion loci for $\dot{y} = 0$ can be determined. Note, that we did not make any statements whether the maxima of the zero-motion loci (with respect to x and y, respectively) are to the left or to the right of the intersection point (x^*, y^*). This, however, is of no importance for the stability properties of the system and can thus safely be ignored.

We can now return to our original question. Assume that two countries begin to trade with each other which are of different size. In the context of the present model, this means that the country with a larger resource base, say, country A, has a higher autarky innovation rate than the other country[6]. As long as both countries do not trade, the lead of country A over country B will continuously be extended and the ratio of differentiated goods will steadily increase and deviate further and further from its trade-BGP value $n^A/n^B = L^A/L^B$. The question we want to answer is: Is it possible to find for every initial ratio of differentiated goods n^A/n^B initial values v^A, v^B such, that the two-country world finds itself on the stable saddle path and thus converges to its long-run BGP?

---

6 The autarky innovation rate of country i is given by $g^i = (1-\theta)L^i - \theta\rho$. If $L^A > L^B$, the innovation rate of country A is greater than in country B.

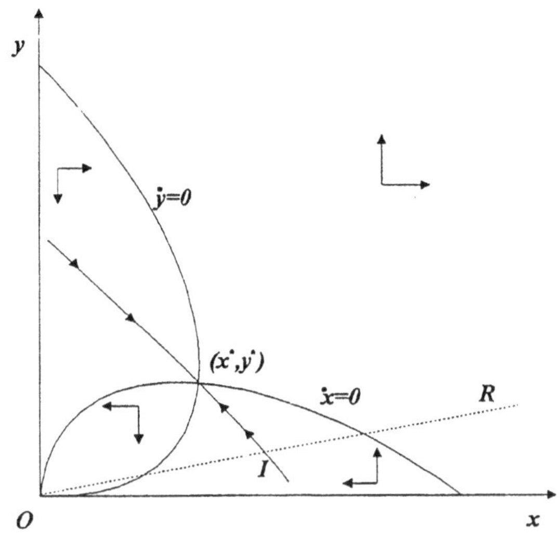

Figure 4.2: Global saddle path stability of the balanced growth path

Remember that the stability analysis of the transformed model is related to the original model by the variable transformation $x := n^A v^B$, $y := n^B v^B$ and $z := v^A / v^B$. Since history dictates initial conditions for n^A and n^B the ratio of x to y is equally given by history and is represented in figure 4.2 by a dashed ray starting from the origin and denoted by OR. Now the question of global stability is equivalent to asking whether we can find values for v^A and v^B such that initial conditions for x and y always lie on the stable saddle path (point I). This, however, is no problem. Varying v^B means moving up and down on OR, thus v^B has simply to be chosen such that initial conditions are indeed given by point I. Then, v^A can be chosen such that $z = 1$ which amounts to saying that $v^A = v^B$. Thus, independently of the initial quantities of differentiated goods in country A and country B, the world economy always converges to its long-run balanced growth path. The system is globally saddle path stable.

Innovation rates

The last subsection has shown that on the stable saddle path, firm values equalize at every moment in time. As a consequence, factor prices equalize by (7) which by

(6) leads to identical goods prices which in turn implies by (5) that the firm size equalizes across countries. A further interesting implication of the model can be shown due to this "firm value equalization": The world as whole is permanently on a balanced growth path. To see this most clearly add the budget constraints of both countries given by (2), divide by world assets A, insert (7), and observe that $v^A = v^B$, $E = 1$ and $r = \rho$, to obtain a world budget constraint which reads (cf. appendix)

$$\frac{\dot{A}}{A} = \rho + L - \frac{1}{A}, \tag{23}$$

where $A = A^A + A^B$ and $L = L^A + L^B$. We know from the analysis of the BGP that in the long-run the total value of all firms is given by $V = 1/(L+\rho)$. Since this value has to equal the value of world assets, the long-run equilibrium value of A is given by that value, too. Equation (23), however, tells us, that this equilibrium value can only be reached if $A = 1/(L+\rho)$ at every moment in time. Since under free trade firms in both countries have the same value, the value of world assets is $A = vn$, where $n = n^A + n^B$, which means that the value of the firms v falls at the same rate as the number of varieties in the world n increases. Computing the world innovation rate then shows (cf. appendix) that this can hold only if it is constant and equal to $g = (1-\theta)L - \theta\rho$. Thus, though innovation rates in countries differ during the adjustment period, new varieties are always introduced, in the world as a whole, at the constant rate of $g = (1-\theta)L - \theta\rho$.

Some results which hold on the BGP can now be transferred to the adjustment period, too: By equation (7), factor rewards are constant and therefore, prices for final goods and plant size are constant, too (and, of course, equalized across countries, as argued above). What adjusts, however, is the ratio of varieties to labour endowment and consequently, innovation rates. In autarky, the innovation rate of the bigger country is higher which is shown in figure 4.3 for the period before t_{trade} when countries open up to trade. Then, during the adjustment period, the innovation rate of country A and country B approach the BGP innovation rate asymptotically. Given the definition of x and y, the innovation rates of country A and B are

$$\frac{\dot{n}^A}{n^A} = \frac{\dot{x}}{x} - \frac{\dot{v}^B}{v^B} = \frac{\dot{x}}{x} - \frac{\dot{v}}{v} = \frac{\dot{x}}{x} + g \quad \text{and} \quad \frac{\dot{n}^B}{n^B} = \frac{\dot{y}}{y} - \frac{\dot{v}}{v} = \frac{\dot{y}}{y} + g,$$

respectively. Further, by the stability analysis we know that x decreases whereas y increases, given that A is the larger country. Thus $\dot{x}/x$ is negative, $\dot{y}/y$ is positive and the innovation rate of country A is always smaller than the long-run innovation rate, whereas the innovation rate of country B approaches its long-run value from above.

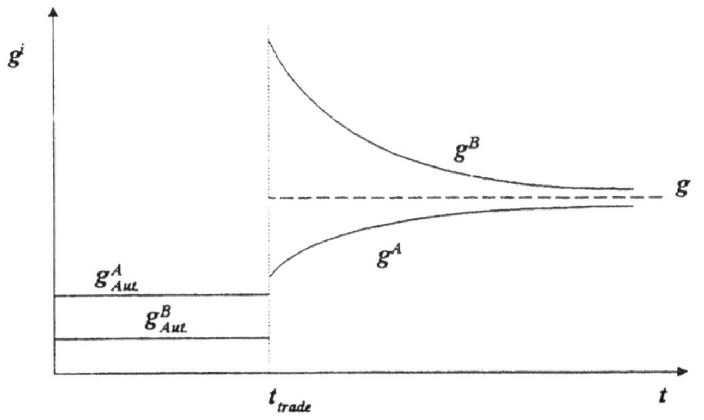

Figure 4.3: Innovation rates before and after opening up to trade

5. International financial capital flows

In the preceding sections, financial capital was assumed to flow freely between countries. We have not yet, however, studied the implications of the degree of capital mobility on ownership and long-run expenditure levels. This will be done in this section.

Solving the budget constraint (2) of a country for $A^i(t)$ yields, by taking the transversality condition (4) into account, the familiar budget constraint which limits the present value of future expenditure at any point in time t by the sum of wealth and the present value of future income,

$$A^i(t)+\int_t^{\infty}\exp\left[-\int_t^{\tau}r(s)ds\right]w^i(\tau)L^i d\tau=\int_t^{\infty}\exp\left[-\int_t^{\tau}r(s)ds\right]E^i(\tau)d\tau.$$

To simplify this expression further, we employ the fact that $r(s)=\rho$ and that the wage rate is given by $w^i = v(n^A + n^B) \equiv V$ which is known, as well as expenditure $E^i = \overline{E}^i$ of country i, to be constant on the stable saddle path. It results that asset holdings of households of country i are constant, too,

$$A^i = \frac{1}{\rho}\left(\overline{E}^i - VL^i\right) = \frac{1}{\rho}\left(\overline{E}^i - \frac{L^i}{L+\rho}\right). \tag{24}$$

The value of firms operating in country i, however, is known to change during the transition period. Given the scenario under consideration, the value of firms of country A, $V^A = n^A v\ (=x)$, falls, whereas the value of firms of country B, $V^B = n^B v\ (=y)$, increases. By the identity $A^i = V^i - D^i$ one therefore knows that debt of country B $\left(D^B = -D^A\right)$ increases over time and converges to a constant long-run BGP value. How fast does this debt increase? Since assets A^B are constant and the value of each firm falls at the world wide innovation rate g, the number of firms owned by households in country B increases at that same rate. This implies that R&D of the "extra" firms created during the catching-up process in country B is entirely financed by households of country A and therefore ownership of those firms lies in country A.

How does this indebtedness relate to long-run expenditure levels? In an identical model with *no* international financial capital flows, long-run expenditure is given by $E^i = L^i/L$; here, however, expenditure is constant and therefore takes the value resulting at the moment of capital flow liberalization, which, in turn depends solely on accumulated savings A^i of the economy under consideration (cf. equation (24)). To illustrate what this means consider two cases: If both countries, before taking up trade in financial capital (but, assume, after having already been trading goods for a while) have the same ratio of firms to labour endowment and therefore are already on their common BGP, no country will borrow from another country, total asset holdings will be given by $A^i = (L+\rho)^{-1} L^i/L$, the expenditure level is $E^i = L^i/L$ and, thus, consumption per capita is equalized. The other extreme is a situation where one country is very far away from the common BGP (assume close to zero firms), then asset holdings are close to zero, expenditure will also be close to zero for all times and no consumption per capita equalization obtains.

This path-dependency of long-run consumption per capita is typical for growth models with international capital flows and similar results are known to hold in a

Ramsey two-country growth model with international capital flows. Thus, it should be borne in mind that convergence in growth rates or factor price equalization does not imply convergence of levels of consumption.

6. Conclusion

We have shown by analytical and graphical means that a model which contains the main features of Grossman-Helpman type models of international trade and growth has a BGP which is locally saddle path stable. Thus small disturbances of the R&D process once the two-country world is on the BGP will be compensated for by the adjustment process. The country with a relatively lower number of differentiated goods will "temporarily" grow faster than the other country. In the long run, both economies converge to the same positive constant innovation rate. In addition to this local stability analysis, we have shown that the system is equally globally saddle path stable. Even countries which differ very much in their number of differentiated goods produced prior to opening up to trade will always find themselves on a saddle path which converges towards the common balanced growth path. By this global stability analysis we could take explicitly into consideration – usually neglected by standard approaches – what happens between autarky and the long-run equilibrium. We found, that the world as a whole is permanently on a balanced growth path which implies that everywhere on the stable saddle path all variables, except the rates of innovation, take already their balanced growth path values: Factor rewards are constant and equalize across countries, as well as prices for differentiated goods and the plant size. Only the rate of innovation of country A and B falls and increases, respectively, to reach a common long-run innovation rate. Thus, on the balanced growth path, both innovation rates and, implicitly, growth rates of consumption per capita equalize in contrast to the level of consumption per capita.

Appendix

1. Local stability of the balanced growth path

Reduced form of the model

Here we derive the reduced form. Solve (7) for w^i and insert it into the pricing equation (6). This yields $p_x^i = v^i n/\theta$. This equation inserted into the aggregated demand function (5), together with $E = E^A + E^B$, results in

$$x^i = \frac{\left(v^i n/\theta\right)^{-\varepsilon}}{n^A\left(v^A n/\theta\right)^{1-\varepsilon} + n^B\left(v^B n/\theta\right)^{1-\varepsilon}} E = \frac{\theta}{n} \frac{\left(v^i\right)^{-\varepsilon}}{n^A\left(v^A\right)^{1-\varepsilon} + n^B\left(v^B\right)^{1-\varepsilon}} E. \tag{A.1}$$

With this equation profits are

$$\pi^i = p^i x^i - w^i x^i = (1-\theta) p^i x^i = (1-\theta) \frac{\left(v^i\right)^{1-\varepsilon}}{n^A\left(v^A\right)^{1-\varepsilon} + n^B\left(v^B\right)^{1-\varepsilon}} E. \tag{A.2}$$

Solving factor market clearing conditions (10) for $\dot{n}^i/n$, inserting the modified demand function as given in (A.1) yields

$$\frac{\dot{n}^i}{n^i}\frac{n^i}{n} = L^i - \frac{n^i}{n} \frac{\theta\left(v^i\right)^{-\varepsilon}}{n^A\left(v^A\right)^{1-\varepsilon} + n^B\left(v^B\right)^{1-\varepsilon}} E.$$

Differentiating (8) with respect to time and inserting (A.2) gives

$$\frac{\dot{v}^i}{v^i} = r - (1-\theta) \frac{\left(v^i\right)^{-\varepsilon}}{n^A\left(v^A\right)^{1-\varepsilon} + n^B\left(v^B\right)^{1-\varepsilon}} E.$$

Walras' Law

The budget constraint (BC) of country i is given by $E^i + \dot{A}^i = rA^i + w^i L^i$. Adding the BC of country A to the BC of country B gives

$$E + \dot{A} = rA + w^A L^A + w^B L^B. \tag{A.3}$$

From (9) we know $\dot{A} = \dot{n}^A v^A + n^A \dot{v}^A + \dot{n}^B v^B + n^B \dot{v}^B$. Inserting (11) and (12) results in

$$\dot{A} = nv^A L^A - \frac{\theta n^A (v^A)^{1-\varepsilon}}{n^A (v^A)^{1-\varepsilon} + n^B (v^B)^{1-\varepsilon}} E + n^A v^A r - (1-\theta) \frac{n^A (v^A)^{1-\varepsilon}}{n^A (v^A)^{1-\varepsilon} + n^B (v^B)^{1-\varepsilon}} E$$

$$+ nv^B L^B - \frac{\theta n^B (v^B)^{1-\varepsilon}}{n^A (v^A)^{1-\varepsilon} + n^B (v^B)^{1-\varepsilon}} E + n^B v^B r - (1-\theta) \frac{n^B (v^B)^{1-\varepsilon}}{n^A (v^A)^{1-\varepsilon} + n^B (v^B)^{1-\varepsilon}} E$$

$$= n\left(v^A L^A + v^B L^B\right) + \left(n^A v^A + n^B v^B\right) r - E.$$

Inserting this expression and equation (7) into (A.3) gives

$$E + n\left(v^A L^A + v^B L^B\right) + \left(n^A v^A + n^B v^B\right) r - E = rA + n\left(v^A L^A + v^B L^B\right).$$

This equation is always fulfilled which means that Walras' Law is satisfied: If one BC holds, the other holds automatically.

Interest rates

Total expenditure $E = E^A + E^B$ is normalized to unity. This implies $\dot{E}^A + \dot{E}^B = 0$. With equation (3) this becomes $(r-\rho)\left(E^A + E^B\right) = 0$ and consequently $r = \rho$.

Balanced growth path

We first solve the system for the BGP and determine its innovation rate. Replace $\dot{n}^i / n^i$ and $-\dot{v}^i / v^i$ by g to get

$$g\frac{n^i}{n} = L^i - \frac{n^i}{n} \frac{\theta (v^i)^{-\varepsilon}}{n^A (v^A)^{1-\varepsilon} + n^B (v^B)^{1-\varepsilon}}, \qquad -g = \rho - (1-\theta) \frac{(v^i)^{-\varepsilon}}{n^A (v^A)^{1-\varepsilon} + n^B (v^B)^{1-\varepsilon}}.$$

Subtract the second equation from itself $(i = A, B)$ and find $v^A = v^B =: v$. Inserting this into the above equations and rearranging gives

$$g = L^i \frac{n}{n^i} - \frac{\theta}{nv}, \qquad g = \frac{1-\theta}{nv} - \rho.$$

From the first equation we can be readily deduce that on the BGP $n^A/L^A = n^B/L^B$ $\Leftrightarrow n^B = n^A\, L^B/L^A$.

Insert this equation into $(n^A/n)+(n^B/n)=1$ and find $(n^A/n)(1+L^B/L^A)=1$. This is equivalent to $n^A/n = L^A/L$ or, more generally

$$n^i/n = L^i/L, \tag{A.4}$$

where $L = L^A + L^B$. Then, solving the first equation for nv

$$g = L - \frac{\theta}{nv} \Leftrightarrow \frac{\theta}{nv} = L - g \Leftrightarrow nv = \frac{\theta}{L-g}, \tag{A.5}$$

and inserting this result into the second gives a positive innovation rate

$$g = \frac{1-\theta}{\theta}(L-g) - \rho \Leftrightarrow g\left(1+\frac{1-\theta}{\theta}\right) = \frac{1-\theta}{\theta}L - \rho \Leftrightarrow g = (1-\theta)L - \theta\rho, \tag{A.6}$$

provided, e.g., the world economy is large or patient enough which is assumed in the following. The value of all firms amounts to

$$nv = \frac{\theta}{L-g} = \frac{\theta}{L-(1-\theta)L+\theta\rho} = \frac{1}{L+\rho}$$

and the value of firms in country i is given by

$$n^i v = nv\frac{n^i}{n} = \frac{1}{L+\rho}\frac{L^i}{L}.$$

Eigenvalues of a substitute-model

Here we first derive the substitute-model (S), then linearize it around its stationary state values and thus obtain its Jacobian J. Finally we compute the eigenvalues of the Jacobian.

The reduced form of the original model is

$$\frac{\dot{n}^A}{n^A} = \frac{n}{n^A}L^A - \frac{\theta\left(v^A\right)^{-\varepsilon}}{n^A\left(v^A\right)^{1-\varepsilon}+n^B\left(v^B\right)^{1-\varepsilon}}, \qquad \frac{\dot{n}^B}{n^B} = \frac{n}{n^B}L^B - \frac{\theta\left(v^B\right)^{-\varepsilon}}{n^A\left(v^A\right)^{1-\varepsilon}+n^B\left(v^B\right)^{1-\varepsilon}},$$

$$\frac{\dot{v}^A(t)}{v^A(t)} = \rho - \frac{(1-\theta)\left(v^A\right)^{-\varepsilon}}{n^A\left(v^A\right)^{1-\varepsilon}+n^B\left(v^B\right)^{1-\varepsilon}}, \qquad \frac{\dot{v}^B(t)}{v^B(t)} = \rho - \frac{(1-\theta)\left(v^B\right)^{-\varepsilon}}{n^A\left(v^A\right)^{1-\varepsilon}+n^B\left(v^B\right)^{1-\varepsilon}}.$$

Define new variables according to

$$x = n^A v^B, \qquad y = n^B v^B, \qquad z = v^A / v^B . \tag{A.7}$$

Then $\dot{x}/x = (\dot{n}^A/n^A) + (\dot{v}^B/v^B)$, $\dot{y}/y = (\dot{n}^B/n^B) + (\dot{v}^B/v^B)$ and $\dot{z}/z = (\dot{v}^A/v^A) - (\dot{v}^B/v^B)$. In full length

$$\frac{\dot{x}}{x} = \frac{n}{n^A} L^A - \frac{\theta (v^A)^{-\varepsilon}}{n^A (v^A)^{1-\varepsilon} + n^B (v^B)^{1-\varepsilon}} + \rho - (1-\theta) \frac{(v^B)^{-\varepsilon}}{n^A (v^A)^{1-\varepsilon} + n^B (v^B)^{1-\varepsilon}},$$

$$\frac{\dot{y}}{y} = \frac{n}{n^B} L^B - \frac{\theta (v^B)^{-\varepsilon}}{n^A (v^A)^{1-\varepsilon} + n^B (v^B)^{1-\varepsilon}} + \rho - (1-\theta) \frac{(v^B)^{-\varepsilon}}{n^A (v^A)^{1-\varepsilon} + n^B (v^B)^{1-\varepsilon}},$$

$$\frac{\dot{z}}{z} = (1-\theta) \frac{(v^B)^{-\varepsilon}}{n^A (v^A)^{1-\varepsilon} + n^B (v^B)^{1-\varepsilon}} - (1-\theta) \frac{(v^A)^{-\varepsilon}}{n^A (v^A)^{1-\varepsilon} + n^B (v^B)^{1-\varepsilon}} .$$

The equations can be simplified to

$$\frac{\dot{x}}{x} = \frac{n}{n^A} L^A + \rho - \frac{(v^B)^{-\varepsilon} + \theta \left((v^A)^{-\varepsilon} - (v^B)^{-\varepsilon} \right)}{n^A (v^A)^{1-\varepsilon} + n^B (v^B)^{1-\varepsilon}},$$

$$\frac{\dot{y}}{y} = \frac{n}{n^B} L^B + \rho - \frac{(v^B)^{-\varepsilon}}{n^A (v^A)^{1-\varepsilon} + n^B (v^B)^{1-\varepsilon}},$$

$$\frac{\dot{z}}{z} = (1-\theta) \frac{(v^B)^{-\varepsilon} - (v^A)^{-\varepsilon}}{n^A (v^A)^{1-\varepsilon} + n^B (v^B)^{1-\varepsilon}} .$$

Now we have to replace the variables of the original system. The procedure is best seen by first rewriting the equations as

$$\frac{\dot{x}}{x} = \left(1 + \frac{n^B}{n^A} \right) L^A + \rho - \frac{1 + \theta \left((v^A/v^B)^{-\varepsilon} - 1 \right)}{n^A v^A (v^A/v^B)^{-\varepsilon} + n^B v^B},$$

$$\frac{\dot{y}}{y} = \left(\frac{n^A}{n^B} + 1 \right) L^B + \rho - \frac{1}{n^A v^A (v^A/v^B)^{-\varepsilon} + n^B v^B},$$

$$\frac{\dot{z}}{z} = (1-\theta) \frac{1 - (v^A/v^B)^{-\varepsilon}}{n^A v^A (v^A/v^B)^{-\varepsilon} + n^B v^B} .$$

Now insert the new variables

$$\frac{\dot{x}}{x}=\left(1+\frac{y}{x}\right)L^A+\rho-\frac{1+\theta\left(z^{-\varepsilon}-1\right)}{xz^{1-\varepsilon}+y},\qquad \frac{\dot{y}}{y}=\left(\frac{x}{y}+1\right)L^B+\rho-\frac{1}{xz^{1-\varepsilon}+y},$$

$$\frac{\dot{z}}{z}=\left(1-\theta\right)\frac{1-z^{-\varepsilon}}{xz^{1-\varepsilon}+y}.$$

Multiplication finally yields the new model (S) as given in the main text:

$$\dot{x}=\left(x+y\right)L^A+\rho x-\frac{1+\theta\left(z^{-\varepsilon}-1\right)}{z^{1-\varepsilon}+yx^{-1}},\qquad \dot{y}=\left(x+y\right)L^B+\rho y-\frac{1}{xy^{-1}z^{1-\varepsilon}+1},$$

$$\dot{z}=\left(1-\theta\right)\frac{z-z^{1-\varepsilon}}{xz^{1-\varepsilon}+y}.$$

Equilibrium values

From the original system we can derive the equilibrium values $\left(x^*,y^*,z^*\right)$ for x, y and z. Inserting (A.6) into (A.5) gives

$$nv=\frac{\theta}{L-\left(\left(1-\theta\right)L-\theta\rho\right)}=\frac{1}{L+\rho}.$$

With $n^i/n=L^i/\left(L^A+L^B\right)$, they are

$$x^*=n^Av^B=\frac{n^A}{n}nv=\frac{1}{L+\rho}\frac{L^A}{L},\qquad y^*=n^Bv^B=n^Bv=\frac{1}{L+\rho}\frac{L^B}{L},$$

$$z^*=1. \tag{A.8}$$

This can be easily verified by inserting them into the transformed system.

$$\dot{x}=\frac{L^A}{L+\rho}+\rho\frac{1}{L+\rho}\frac{L^A}{L}-\frac{1}{1+L^B/L^A}=\frac{L^A}{L+\rho}+\rho\frac{1}{L+\rho}\frac{L^A}{L}-\frac{L^A}{L}$$

$$=\frac{L^A}{L+\rho}\left(1+\frac{\rho}{L}\right)-\frac{L^A}{L}=\frac{L^A}{L+\rho}\frac{L+\rho}{L}-\frac{L^A}{L}=0,$$

$$\dot{y}=\frac{L^B}{L+\rho}+\rho\frac{1}{L+\rho}\frac{L^B}{L}-\frac{1}{L^A/L^B+1}=\frac{L^B}{L+\rho}\left(1+\frac{\rho}{L}\right)-\frac{L^B}{L}=0,$$

$$\dot{z}=\left(1-\theta\right)\frac{1-1}{x^*+y^*}=0.$$

Jacobian

The Jacobian is obtained by linearizing the transformed system (S) and evaluating it at its equilibrium values (x^*, y^*, z^*).

$$\frac{\partial \dot{x}}{\partial x} = L^A + \rho + \frac{1+\theta(z^{-\varepsilon}-1)}{(z^{1-\varepsilon}+yx^{-1})^2}(-yx^{-2}), \qquad \frac{\partial \dot{x}}{\partial y} = L^A + \frac{1+\theta(z^{-\varepsilon}-1)}{(z^{1-\varepsilon}+yx^{-1})^2}x^{-1},$$

$$\frac{\partial \dot{x}}{\partial z} = -\frac{\theta(-\varepsilon)z^{-\varepsilon-1}(z^{1-\varepsilon}+yx^{-1})-(1+\theta(z^{-\varepsilon}-1))(1-\varepsilon)z^{-\varepsilon}}{(z^{1-\varepsilon}+yx^{-1})^2},$$

$$\frac{\partial \dot{y}}{\partial x} = L^B + \frac{y^{-1}z^{1-\varepsilon}}{(xy^{-1}z^{1-\varepsilon}+1)^2}, \qquad \frac{\partial \dot{y}}{\partial y} = L^B + \rho + \frac{1}{(xy^{-1}z^{1-\varepsilon}+1)^2}(-xy^{-2}z^{1-\varepsilon}),$$

$$\frac{\partial \dot{y}}{\partial z} = \frac{(1-\varepsilon)xy^{-1}z^{-\varepsilon}}{(xy^{-1}z^{1-\varepsilon}+1)^2}, \qquad \frac{\partial \dot{z}}{\partial x} = -(1-\theta)\frac{z-z^{1-\varepsilon}}{(xz^{1-\varepsilon}+y)^2}z^{1-\varepsilon},$$

$$\frac{\partial \dot{z}}{\partial y} = -(1-\theta)\frac{z-z^{1-\varepsilon}}{(xz^{1-\varepsilon}+y)^2},$$

$$\frac{\partial \dot{z}}{\partial z} = (1-\theta)\frac{(1-(1-\varepsilon)z^{-\varepsilon})(xz^{1-\varepsilon}+y)-(z-z^{1-\varepsilon})x(1-\varepsilon)z^{-\varepsilon}}{(xz^{1-\varepsilon}+y)^2},$$

These equations simplify tremendously when evaluated at the equilibrium values (x^*, y^*, z^*). One obtains:

$$\frac{\partial \dot{x}}{\partial x} = L^A + \rho - \frac{y^*}{(x^*+y^*)^2} = L^A + \rho - \frac{(L+\rho)L^B}{L} = L^A + \rho - \left(1+\frac{\rho}{L}\right)L^B,$$

$$\frac{\partial \dot{x}}{\partial y} = L^A + \frac{x^*}{(x^*+y^*)^2} = L^A + (L+\rho)\frac{L^A}{L} = L^A\left(2+\frac{\rho}{L}\right),$$

$$\frac{\partial \dot{x}}{\partial z} = -\frac{-\varepsilon\theta(1+L^B/L^A)-(1-\varepsilon)}{(1+L^B/L^A)^2} = \frac{\theta}{1-\theta}\frac{L^A}{L} - \frac{\theta}{1-\theta}\left(\frac{L^A}{L}\right)^2 = \frac{\theta}{1-\theta}\frac{L^A}{L}\frac{L^B}{L},$$

$$\frac{\partial \dot{y}}{\partial x} = L^B + \frac{L+\rho}{(L^A/L^B+1)^2}\frac{L}{L^B} = L^B + (L+\rho)\frac{L^B}{L} = 2L^B + \rho\frac{L^B}{L} = L^B\left(2+\frac{\rho}{L}\right),$$

$$\frac{\partial \dot{y}}{\partial y} = L^B + \rho - \frac{x^*}{(x^*+y^*)^2} = L^B + \rho - \frac{1}{L+\rho}\frac{L^A}{L}(L+\rho)^2 = L^B + \rho - (L+\rho)\frac{L^A}{L}$$

$$= L^B + \rho - \left(1+\frac{\rho}{L}\right)L^A,$$

$$\frac{\partial \dot{y}}{\partial z}=\frac{(1-\varepsilon)x^{*}y^{*}}{\left(x^{*}+y^{*}\right)^{2}}=(1-\varepsilon)\frac{L^{A}L^{B}L^{-2}}{(L+\rho)^{2}}(L+\rho)^{2}=(1-\varepsilon)\frac{L^{A}L^{B}}{L^{2}}=\frac{-\theta}{1-\theta}\frac{L^{A}L^{B}}{L^{2}},$$

$$\frac{\partial \dot{z}}{\partial x}=\frac{\partial \dot{z}}{\partial y}=0,$$

$$\frac{\partial \dot{z}}{\partial z}=(1-\theta)\frac{\varepsilon\left(x^{*}+y^{*}\right)}{\left(x^{*}+y^{*}\right)^{2}}=\frac{1}{x^{*}+y^{*}}=L+\rho.$$

The Jacobian, therefore, is

$$J=\begin{pmatrix} L^{A}+\rho-\left(1+\frac{\rho}{L}\right)L^{B} & L^{A}\left(2+\frac{\rho}{L}\right) & \frac{\theta}{1-\theta}\frac{L^{A}L^{B}}{L^{2}} \\ L^{B}\left(2+\frac{\rho}{L}\right) & L^{B}+\rho-\left(1+\frac{\rho}{L}\right)L^{A} & \frac{-\theta}{1-\theta}\frac{L^{A}L^{B}}{L^{2}} \\ 0 & 0 & L+\rho \end{pmatrix}.$$

Eigenvalues

The eigenvalues λ of this matrix can be found by solving $|J-\lambda I|=0$, where I is the identity matrix. Expansion by the last row of $|J-\lambda I|$ gives

$$[L+\rho-\lambda]\left[\left(L^{A}+\rho-\left(1+\frac{\rho}{L}\right)L^{B}-\lambda\right)\left(L^{B}+\rho-\left(1+\frac{\rho}{L}\right)L^{A}-\lambda\right)-L^{A}L^{B}\left(2+\frac{\rho}{L}\right)^{2}\right].$$

Thus the first eigenvalue is given by $\lambda_1 = L+\rho$. The others are determined by

$$\left(L^{A}+\rho-\left(1+\frac{\rho}{L}\right)L^{B}-\lambda\right)\left(L^{B}+\rho-\left(1+\frac{\rho}{L}\right)L^{A}-\lambda\right)-L^{A}L^{B}\left(2+\frac{\rho}{L}\right)^{2}=0\Leftrightarrow$$

$$\left(L^{A}+\rho-\left(1+\frac{\rho}{L}\right)L^{B}\right)\left(L^{B}+\rho-\left(1+\frac{\rho}{L}\right)L^{A}\right)$$
$$-\lambda\left(L^{A}+\rho-\left(1+\frac{\rho}{L}\right)L^{B}\right)-\lambda\left(L^{B}+\rho-\left(1+\frac{\rho}{L}\right)L^{A}\right)+\lambda^{2}-L^{A}L^{B}\left(1+\left(1+\frac{\rho}{L}\right)\right)^{2}=0\Leftrightarrow$$

$$L^{A}L^{B}+L^{A}\rho-\left(1+\frac{\rho}{L}\right)L^{A^{2}}+\rho L^{B}+\rho^{2}-\left(1+\frac{\rho}{L}\right)\rho L^{A}$$
$$-\left(1+\frac{\rho}{L}\right)L^{B^{2}}-\left(1+\frac{\rho}{L}\right)L^{B}\rho+\left(1+\frac{\rho}{L}\right)^{2}L^{A}L^{B}$$
$$-\lambda\rho+\lambda^{2}-L^{A}L^{B}-2L^{A}L^{B}\left(1+\frac{\rho}{L}\right)-L^{A}L^{B}\left(1+\frac{\rho}{L}\right)^{2}=0\Leftrightarrow$$

$$L^A\rho-\left(1+\frac{\rho}{L}\right)\left(L^{A2}+L^{B2}+2L^AL^B+\rho L^A+L^B\rho\right)+\rho L^B+\rho^2-\lambda\rho+\lambda^2=0\Leftrightarrow$$

$$-\left(1+\frac{\rho}{L}\right)L(L+\rho)+\rho(L+\rho)-\lambda\rho+\lambda^2=0\Leftrightarrow$$

$$\lambda^2-\lambda\rho-L(L+\rho)=0\Leftrightarrow\lambda_2=L+\rho,\ \lambda_3=-L.$$

Thus the eigenvalues are given by $\lambda_{1,2}=L+\rho$ and $\lambda_3=-L$.

Transitional dynamics and convergence

The eigenvector f_i is determined by $(J-\lambda_i I)f_i=0$. Since we have two equal roots $(\lambda_1=\lambda_2)$, matrix J may not have three linearly independent eigenvectors (for a detailed discussion of what should be done in that case, see Braun, 1975). Here, however, we do find two linearly independent eigenvectors for eigenvalues $\lambda_1=\lambda_2$ which can be computed as follows.

$$(J-\lambda_{1,2}I)f_{1,2}=0\Leftrightarrow$$

$$\begin{pmatrix} L^A+\rho-\left(1+\frac{\rho}{L}\right)L^B-L-\rho & L^A\left(2+\frac{\rho}{L}\right) & \frac{\theta}{1-\theta}\frac{L^AL^B}{L^2} \\ L^B\left(2+\frac{\rho}{L}\right) & L^B+\rho-\left(1+\frac{\rho}{L}\right)L^A-L-\rho & \frac{-\theta}{1-\theta}\frac{L^AL^B}{L^2} \\ 0 & 0 & 0 \end{pmatrix}f_{1,2}=0\Leftrightarrow$$

$$\begin{pmatrix} -L^B\left(2+\frac{\rho}{L}\right) & L^A\left(2+\frac{\rho}{L}\right) & \frac{\theta}{1-\theta}\frac{L^AL^B}{L^2} \\ L^B\left(2+\frac{\rho}{L}\right) & -L^A\left(2+\frac{\rho}{L}\right) & \frac{-\theta}{1-\theta}\frac{L^AL^B}{L^2} \\ 0 & 0 & 0 \end{pmatrix}f_{1,2}=0.$$

This is solved by the non-zero vectors

$$f_1=c_1\left(1/L^B,1/L^A,0\right)^T,\qquad f_2=c_2\left(0,\frac{1}{L^A(2+\rho/L)},-\frac{1-\theta}{\theta}\frac{L^2}{L^AL^B}\right)^T.$$

where c_i are arbitrary constants.

The third eigenvector is given by

$$(J-\lambda_3 I)f_3 = 0 \Leftrightarrow$$

$$\begin{pmatrix} L^A+\rho-\left(1+\frac{\rho}{L}\right)L^B+L & L^A\left(2+\frac{\rho}{L}\right) & \frac{\theta}{1-\theta}\frac{L^A L^B}{L^2} \\ L^B\left(2+\frac{\rho}{L}\right) & L^B+\rho-\left(1+\frac{\rho}{L}\right)L^A+L & \frac{-\theta}{1-\theta}\frac{L^A L^B}{L^2} \\ 0 & 0 & L+\rho+L \end{pmatrix} f_3 = 0 \Leftrightarrow$$

$$\begin{pmatrix} 2L^A+\rho-L^B\frac{\rho}{L} & L^A\left(2+\frac{\rho}{L}\right) & \frac{\theta}{1-\theta}\frac{L^A L^B}{L^2} \\ L^B\left(2+\frac{\rho}{L}\right) & 2L^B+\rho-L^A\frac{\rho}{L} & \frac{-\theta}{1-\theta}\frac{L^A L^B}{L^2} \\ 0 & 0 & 2L+\rho \end{pmatrix} f_3 = 0.$$

This is equivalent to, by adding a suitable multiple of the third row to the first and second, and adding the second to the first,

$$\begin{pmatrix} 2L+\rho & 2L+\rho & 0 \\ L^B\left(2+\frac{\rho}{L}\right) & 2L^B+\rho-L^A\frac{\rho}{L} & 0 \\ 0 & 0 & 2L+\rho \end{pmatrix} f_3 = 0.$$

A solution to this is given by $f_3 = c_3(1,-1,0)^T$. Thus the general solution to $(\dot{\tilde{x}},\dot{\tilde{y}},\dot{\tilde{z}})^T = J(\tilde{x},\tilde{y},\tilde{z})^T$ reads

$$\begin{pmatrix} \tilde{x} \\ \tilde{y} \\ \tilde{z} \end{pmatrix} = c_1\begin{pmatrix} \frac{1}{L^B} \\ \frac{1}{L^A} \\ 0 \end{pmatrix}\exp[(L+\rho)t] + c_2\begin{pmatrix} 0 \\ \frac{1}{L^A(2+\rho/L)} \\ -\frac{1-\theta}{\theta}\frac{L^2}{L^A L^B} \end{pmatrix}\exp[(L+\rho)t] + c_3\begin{pmatrix} 1 \\ -1 \\ 0 \end{pmatrix}\exp[-Lt].$$

Time paths on the saddle path and deriving equation (20)

The constants c_i are determined by initial conditions, which are assumed to be given as $\tilde{\psi}(0) = \tilde{\psi}_0$, $\psi = x, y, z$. Constants are then determined by

$$\tilde{x}_0 = \frac{c_1}{L^B}+c_3,\quad \tilde{y}_0 = \frac{c_1}{L^A}+\frac{c_2}{L^A(2+\rho/L)}-c_3,\quad \tilde{z}_0 = -c_2\frac{1-\theta}{\theta}\frac{L^2}{L^A L^B}.$$

Thus $c_2 = -\tilde{z}_0 \frac{\theta}{1-\theta} \frac{L^A L^B}{L^2}$ and $-c_3 = \frac{c_1}{L^B} - \tilde{x}_0$. (A.9)

Hence,

$$\tilde{y}_0 = \frac{c_1}{L^A} - \tilde{z}_0 \frac{\theta}{1-\theta} \frac{L^B}{L(2L+\rho)} + \frac{c_1}{L^B} - \tilde{x}_0 \Leftrightarrow$$

$$c_1 = \left(\tilde{y}_0 + \tilde{z}_0 \frac{\theta}{1-\theta} \frac{L^B}{L(2L+\rho)} + \tilde{x}_0 \right) \left(\frac{1}{L^A} + \frac{1}{L^B} \right)^{-1}. \tag{A.10}$$

and consequently

$$c_3 = -\frac{1}{L^B} \left(\tilde{y}_0 + \tilde{z}_0 \frac{\theta}{1-\theta} \frac{L^B}{L(2L+\rho)} + \tilde{x}_0 \right) \left(\frac{1}{L^A} + \frac{1}{L^B} \right)^{-1} + \tilde{x}_0. \tag{A.11}$$

Initial conditions $\tilde{\psi}(t_0) = \tilde{\psi}_0$, in turn, have to be chosen such, that the system lies on its stable saddle path. This requires c_1 and c_2 to be zero. Thus by (A.9)

$$\tilde{z}_0 = 0, \tag{A.12}$$

and by (A.10)

$$0 = \tilde{y}_0 + \tilde{x}_0 \Leftrightarrow \tilde{y}_0 = -\tilde{x}_0. \tag{A.13}$$

The third constant is then given by (A.11) as

$$c_3 = \tilde{x}_0,$$

and the trajectories on the linearized, stable saddle path are given by

$$\begin{pmatrix} \tilde{x} \\ \tilde{y} \\ \tilde{z} \end{pmatrix} = \tilde{x}_0 \begin{pmatrix} 1 \\ -1 \\ 0 \end{pmatrix} \exp[-Lt].$$

In order to see more clearly what this implies in terms of the original model, we re-transform variables, defined in (A.7). Note that

$$\tilde{\psi} = \psi - \psi^*, \qquad \psi = x, y, z, \tag{A.14}$$

where ψ^* are given by (A.8). Thus choosing $\tilde{z}_0 = 0$ means by (A.14) choosing z such that $z = z^* = 1$. In terms of the original variables, conditions on initial values (A.12) and (A.13) read

$$v_0^A / v_0^B = 1$$

$$y_0 - y^* = -\left(x_0 - x^*\right) \Leftrightarrow n_0^B v_0^B - \frac{1}{L+\rho}\frac{L^B}{L} = -\left(n_0^A v_0^B - \frac{1}{L+\rho}\frac{L^A}{L}\right) \Leftrightarrow$$

$$\Leftrightarrow \left(n_0^B + n_0^A\right) v_0^B = \frac{1}{L+\rho}.$$

Since both n_0^A and n_0^B, as state variables, are given by history, these conditions are equivalent to saying that v_0^A and v_0^B have to be chosen at t_0 such that

$$v_0^A = v_0^B = \frac{1}{\left(n_0^B + n_0^A\right)\left(L+\rho\right)}.$$

Thus, the trajectories on the saddle path read in terms of "original" variables

$$\begin{pmatrix} \tilde{x} \\ \tilde{y} \\ \tilde{z} \end{pmatrix} = \left(x_0 - x^*\right) \begin{pmatrix} 1 \\ -1 \\ 0 \end{pmatrix} \exp[-Lt] = \left(\frac{n_0^A}{\left(n_0^B + n_0^A\right)\left(L+\rho\right)} - \frac{1}{L+\rho}\frac{L^A}{L} \right) \begin{pmatrix} 1 \\ -1 \\ 0 \end{pmatrix} \exp[-Lt] =$$

$$= \frac{1}{L+\rho}\left(\frac{n_0^A}{n_0^B + n_0^A} - \frac{L^A}{L} \right) \begin{pmatrix} 1 \\ -1 \\ 0 \end{pmatrix} \exp[-Lt], \qquad \text{(A.15)}$$

which implies that no transitional dynamics are observed if $\frac{n_0^A}{n_0^B + n_0^A} = \frac{L^A}{L}$. This, however, makes perfectly sense, since this condition was identified as a characteristic of the BGP in (A.4).

Computing equation (21)

By (A.14), (A.7) and (A.8)

$$\tilde{x} = n^A v^B - \frac{1}{L+\rho}\frac{L^A}{L}, \qquad \tilde{y} = n^B v^B - \frac{1}{L+\rho}\frac{L^B}{L}.$$

Thus, with identical firm values denoted by v,

$$n^A = \left(\tilde{x} + \frac{1}{L+\rho}\frac{L^A}{L}\right) v^{-1}, \qquad n^B = \left(\tilde{y} + \frac{1}{L+\rho}\frac{L^B}{L}\right) v^{-1}.$$

With (A.15) and after multiplying numerator and denominator by $L+\rho$ we obtain equation (21).

2. Global stability properties and innovation rates

Global stability

We prove (cf. remark in footnote 5 of section 4) that the value of firms in country A and country B must be identical on a path leading to a long-run equilibrium.

If firm values differed (assume, without loss of generality $v^A > v^B$) then $\dot{v}^A/v^A > \dot{v}^B/v^B$ $\forall$ t, since

$$\dot{v}^A/v^A > \dot{v}^B/v^B \Leftrightarrow$$

$$\rho-(1-\theta)\frac{\left(v^A\right)^{-\varepsilon}}{n^A\left(v^A\right)^{1-\varepsilon}+n^B\left(v^B\right)^{1-\varepsilon}} > \rho-(1-\theta)\frac{\left(v^B\right)^{-\varepsilon}}{n^A\left(v^A\right)^{1-\varepsilon}+n^B\left(v^B\right)^{1-\varepsilon}} \Leftrightarrow$$

$$\frac{\left(v^B\right)^{-\varepsilon}}{n^A\left(v^A\right)^{1-\varepsilon}+n^B\left(v^B\right)^{1-\varepsilon}} > \frac{\left(v^A\right)^{-\varepsilon}}{n^A\left(v^A\right)^{1-\varepsilon}+n^B\left(v^B\right)^{1-\varepsilon}} \Leftrightarrow \left(v^B\right)^{-\varepsilon} > \left(v^A\right)^{-\varepsilon} \Leftrightarrow$$

$$\left(v^A\right)^{\varepsilon} > \left(v^B\right)^{\varepsilon} \Leftrightarrow v^A > v^B, \text{ since } \varepsilon > 1.$$

If $\dot{v}^A/v^A > \dot{v}^B/v^B$ and $v^A > v^B$, however, firm values will never equalize if they differ only once. Thus, since on the BGP $v^A = v^B$, a necessary condition that the world economy reaches its long-run equilibrium is that firm values of trading economies equalize at every moment in time.

Innovation rates

Add the budget constraints of both countries given by (2) to obtain $E + \dot{A} = rA + w^A L^A + w^B L^B$. Dividing by world assets A, inserting (7) and observing that $v^A = v^B$, gives $\frac{E}{A}+\frac{\dot{A}}{A} = r + L^A + L^B$. Since world expenditure is normalized at unity and, therefore, $r = \rho$, we obtain $\frac{\dot{A}}{A} = \rho + L - \frac{1}{A}$.

World innovation rate

We show here that a constant value of world assets A implies that new varieties in the world as a whole are permanently introduced at a rate of $g = (1-\theta)L - \theta\rho$.

We can express the world innovation rate as

$$\frac{\dot{n}}{n} = \frac{\dot{n}^A}{n} + \frac{\dot{n}^B}{n} = \frac{\dot{n}^A}{n^A}\frac{n^A}{n} + \frac{\dot{n}^B}{n^B}\frac{n^B}{n}$$

$$= L^A - \frac{n^A}{n}\frac{\theta\left(v^A\right)^{-\varepsilon}}{n^A\left(v^A\right)^{1-\varepsilon} + n^B\left(v^B\right)^{1-\varepsilon}} + L^B - \frac{n^B}{n}\frac{\theta\left(v^B\right)^{-\varepsilon}}{n^A\left(v^A\right)^{1-\varepsilon} + n^B\left(v^B\right)^{1-\varepsilon}} = L - \frac{\theta}{nv}.$$

The evolution of the value of the firms is given by ($v^A = v^B$!)

$$\frac{\dot{v}}{v} = \rho - \frac{1-\theta}{nv}.$$

Since $A = vn = const.$, where $n = n^A + n^B$, these two equations can be only fulfilled if $\dot{n}/n = -\dot{v}/v = g = (1-\theta)L - \theta\rho$.

3. International capital flows

Expenditure of country i

We show here, that in the absence of financial capital flows, expenditure of country i on the BGP is given by $E^i = L^i/L$.

The budget constraint (BC) of country i is given by

$$E^i + \dot{A}^i = rA^i + w_L^i L^i \Leftrightarrow \frac{E^i}{A^i} + \frac{\dot{A}^i}{A^i} = r + \frac{w_L^i L^i}{A^i}.$$

Since capital flows are excluded assets held by consumers of country i amount to the value of firms in country i: $A^i = n^i v^i$. Thus the BC reads

$$\frac{E^i}{n^i v^i} + \frac{\dot{n}^i}{n^i} + \frac{\dot{v}^i}{v^i} = r + \frac{w_L^i L^i}{n^i v^i}.$$

Inserting (7), (11) and (12) results in

$$\frac{E^i}{n^i v^i}+\frac{n}{n^i}L^i-\frac{\theta\left(v^i\right)^{-\varepsilon}}{n^A\left(v^A\right)^{1-\varepsilon}+n^B\left(v^B\right)^{1-\varepsilon}}E+r-(1-\theta)\frac{\left(v^i\right)^{-\varepsilon}}{n^A\left(v^A\right)^{1-\varepsilon}+n^B\left(v^B\right)^{1-\varepsilon}}E=r+\frac{n}{n^i}L^i$$

$$\Leftrightarrow \frac{E^i}{n^i v^i}-\frac{\theta\left(v^i\right)^{-\varepsilon}}{n^A\left(v^A\right)^{1-\varepsilon}+n^B\left(v^B\right)^{1-\varepsilon}}E-(1-\theta)\frac{\left(v^i\right)^{-\varepsilon}}{n^A\left(v^A\right)^{1-\varepsilon}+n^B\left(v^B\right)^{1-\varepsilon}}E=0$$

$$\Leftrightarrow \frac{E^i}{E}=\frac{n^i\left(v^i\right)^{1-\varepsilon}}{n^A\left(v^A\right)^{1-\varepsilon}+n^B\left(v^B\right)^{1-\varepsilon}}.$$

Since world expenditure is normalized to unity $E=1$ and on the balanced growth path $v^A=v^B$ and $n^i/n=L^i/L$, this is equivalent to $E^i=L^i/L$.

Chapter 5: Impatience, factor endowment and trade patterns in a small open economy of endogenous growth

1. Introduction

The pure theory of international trade names various determinants of trade patterns: Apart from differences in technology and preferences or trade due to transportation costs, economies of scale and factor endowments are probably the most prominent ones. The latter is the unique determinant in Heckscher-Ohlin models of two homogenous goods and two factors where the physically relatively capital rich country exports the capital intensive good. Economies of scale can be found in models of intra- and inter-industrial trade (Helpman, 1981; Lawrence and Spiller, 1983; Helpman and Krugman, 1985, ch.7) where the same pattern of trade emerges, except for the fact that now there is a *net* exporter and a *net* importer of the differentiated product, provided that incomplete specialization prevails under free trade. Analogue findings can be provided in a context of endogenous growth, caused by technological spillovers, as was shown by Grossman and Helpman (1991, ch. 7).

Factor richness in these models is measured in terms of physical factor endowment and each country exports the good which makes relative intensive use of the factor which is physically relatively abundant in that country. One condition that this quantity version of the Heckscher-Ohlin theorem holds is that demand functions for final goods are internationally identical. If they differ to such an extend that demand outweighs physical factor abundance (let e.g. the capital rich country have a strong preference for the capital intensive good), the price version of the Heckscher-Ohlin theorem (cf. e.g. Ethier, 1984, p. 141) would have to be applied in order to obtain a correct prediction of trade patterns. Factor richness would then have to be measured in terms of autarky factor rewards.

In the model presented below we derive two further reasons why the trade pattern of a country no longer reflects its physical factor richness. By doing this we introduce a further determinant of trade patterns which so far has attracted less attention in the literature. The analysis will be undertaken in a model of a small open economy of endogenous growth since this allows an easier proof of the results which would not change in a two-country world.

The organization and major findings of the chapter are as follows: The next section presents a small open economy model with two perfectly competitive sectors producing two final homogeneous goods, one monopolistic sector manufacturing intermediate goods and one R&D sector. International capital flows or trade in intermediate goods are ruled out and the economy is assumed to trade in final goods only. The model is similar to Grossman and Helpman (1991, ch. 6) but uses more general production functions. The next section also discusses conditions for a balanced growth path with incomplete specialization. If the economy is too small to sustain positive long-run growth, incomplete specialization requires that the endowment point of the economy lies within a cone of diversification given by world market prices for final goods and production technologies. This condition is well-known from static Heckscher-Ohlin models. For a growing economy, however, the conditions for incomplete specialization is a function of the domestic growth rate and therefore differs considerably from standard results. It is e.g. perfectly possible that one economy is completely specialized though it has an identical endowment ratio capital to labour as another economy which is incompletely specialized. The third section analyzes the impact of factor endowment on trade patterns. We will show that a physically capital rich country which is incompletely specialized when trading can become an exporter of the labour intensive good though capital is its physically relatively abundant factor. This result does not require any differences between the countries apart from factor endowment[1]. It implies that even between countries with identical preferences and identical human capital to labour ratio, inter-industrial trade will be observed. In the fourth section we first investigate the impact of a so far neglected determinant of trade patterns – the time preference rate – and then let the effects caused by differing time preference rates interact with the effects due to factor endowment. It turns out that a country with a fairly impatient population has a tendency to export

1 An alternative reason for such an effect was suggested in a recent paper by Dinopoulos et. al. (1993). By allowing for international trade in assets, they show that trade patterns depend on asset-adjusted endowment rather than physical endowment alone. International capital flows, however, are not necessary for such a situation as will be shown here.

the human capital intensive good. The interaction of impatience[2] and factor endowment effects then extents the result that a capital rich country exports the labour intensive good to a broader range of parameter values and thereby generalizes these findings. Having shown that the quantity version of the Heckscher-Ohlin theorem can no longer be applied to obtain a correct prediction of trade patterns, the subsequent section will show that the results are in accordance with standard trade theory if the price version of the Heckscher-Ohlin theorem is used to measure capital richness. We find that in all situations where the quantity version fails each country has indeed a relative comparative advantage in the good it exports if it is measured in autarky factor rewards. A final section concludes the findings and gives an outlook.

2. A small open economy

Production side

The economy in consideration is small with respect to the economic environment in which it operates. It is endowed with two primary factors and produces two final goods X and Z, which are traded at exogenously given world market prices p_X and p_Z. Both goods are produced under perfect competition using the two primary factors human capital H and labour L, as well as a set of (non-tradable) intermediate goods i as inputs. Letting D_j, $j = X, Z$, represent an index of the intermediate goods used in sector j, the production function can be expressed by

$$X = X_0 H_Z^{\beta} D_Z^{\eta} L_Z^{1-\eta-\beta}, \quad 0<\beta, \eta, 1-\eta-\beta<1, \tag{1}$$

for the good X and by

$$Z = Z_0 H_Z^{\alpha} D_Z^{\eta} L_Z^{1-\eta-\alpha}, \quad 0<\alpha, \eta, 1-\eta-\alpha<1, \tag{2}$$

for good Z. The output elasticities are assumed to be such ($\beta > \alpha$) that the production of the high-tech good X makes more intensively use of human capital than the food industry Z.

[2] (High) time preference rate, (high) individual discount factor and high impatience will be used synonymously throughout the chapter.

From this constant-returns-to-scale production functions unit cost functions, which must equal prices p_Z and p_X, respectively[3], can be directly derived. With a suitable choice of X_0 and Z_0 they are given by $c_X(\cdot) = w_H^\beta p_D^\eta w_L^{1-\eta-\beta}$ and $c_Z(\cdot) = w_H^\alpha p_D^\eta w_L^{1-\eta-\alpha}$ where w_j, $j = H, L$, are the factor rewards for human capital and labour and p_D is the price of the set of intermediate goods used in production. By applying Shephard's Lemma, unit demand functions for labour, the input index D and human capital can be computed. This gives for good X, with reinserting p_X,

$$b_{HX} = \beta \frac{p_X}{w_H}, \qquad b_{DX} = \eta \frac{p_X}{p_D}, \qquad b_{LX} = (1-\eta-\beta)\frac{p_X}{w_L},$$

and for good Z

$$b_{HZ} = \alpha \frac{p_Z}{w_H}, \qquad b_{DZ} = \eta \frac{p_Z}{p_D}, \qquad b_{LZ} = (1-\eta-\alpha)\frac{p_Z}{w_L}.$$

With the unit demand functions b_{DX} and b_{DZ} for the input index D, we can readily express total demand for D as a function of the quantity of X and Z supplied as

$$D^D = \eta \frac{p_X}{p_D} X^S + \eta \frac{p_Z}{p_D} Z^S. \tag{3}$$

What we do not yet know, however, is, how this input index is specified. We adopt the well-known Dixit-Stiglitz (1977) specification which was introduced — in a similar formulation — into production theory by Ethier (1982). It reads

$$D^S = \left(\int_0^n (y^i)^\theta di \right)^{1/\theta}, \quad 0 < \theta < 1, \tag{4}$$

where n is the (measure of the) number of intermediate goods i available domestically. How will producers in sector X and Z assemble intermediate goods in order to obtain the required quantity of D? The optimal choice results from minimizing total costs $\int_0^n p_y^i y^i di$ with respect to y^i subject to (4). This gives demand for each variety of the form

$$y^i = (p_y^i)^{-\varepsilon} D^S \left(\int_0^n (p_y^i)^{1-\varepsilon} di \right)^{-\varepsilon/(\varepsilon-1)} \tag{5}$$

and a unit cost function, which equals the price p_D both final good sectors have to pay for one unit of D and which reads

$$p_D = c_D(p_y^i) = \left(\int_0^n (p_y^i)^{1-\varepsilon} \right)^{1/(1-\varepsilon)},$$

3 Of course, this holds only if both final goods are produced. Later on in this section we will give conditions for such a situation.

where $\varepsilon = 1/(1-\theta)$ is the elasticity of substitution between any two intermediate goods.

Obviously, before intermediate goods can be used in the production process of final goods, they must be produced. The production function for each intermediate good is $y^i = y_0^i H_{y^i}^{\gamma} L_{y^i}^{1-\gamma}$, $0 < \gamma < 1$. Each producer i faces her "own" demand function given by (5) and maximizes profits accordingly. The resulting profit maximizing price is

$$p_y = \frac{c_D}{\theta} = \frac{w_H^{\gamma} w_L^{1-\gamma}}{\theta}, \qquad (6)$$

which implies equal pricing of all varieties since the production costs do not vary between the single firms of sector Y.

Aggregating all firms of this sector, total demand for primary factors depending on factor rewards and aggregate output Y^S is given by

$$L_Y^D = nb_{LY}(w_L, w_H)y^S = (1-\gamma)(w_H/w_L)^{\gamma} Y^S, \qquad (7)$$

$$H_Y^D = nb_{HY}(w_L, w_H)y^S = \gamma(w_L/w_H)^{1-\gamma} Y^S. \qquad (8)$$

Prior to the production of a variety of the differentiated good, firms have to develop a new blueprint which introduces increasing returns to scale for the firms in sector Y. The R&D process itself requires human capital and labour plus knowledge Kn as production factors and is more human capital intensive than both manufacturing activities. The production function is assumed to exhibit constant-returns-to-scale in human capital and labour but increasing-returns-to-scale in all three factors. As a by-product of the development of new blueprints, non-appropriable knowledge itself is increased (Romer, 1990) which is assumed to be immediately available for the creation of new varieties. Formally, the production function for blueprints is $\dot{n} = f_R(H_R, L_R)Kn$. Knowledge which disseminates only locally[4] (within the country where the new blueprint was developed), is assumed to increase linearly in the measure n for the number of varieties produced and consumed domestically. Thus with a suitable choice of units Kn can be set equal to n. As is well known, it is this technological external effect which leads to positive

[4] This assumption could be relaxed (which would not change the basic results) by allowing for an international flow of knowledge with decreasing returns to scale in foreign knowledge.

long-run growth rates. Under these assumptions, the demand functions for factors per growth-rate unit of $g := \dot{n}/n$ are given by $a_{jR}(w_L, w_H)$, $j = L, H$.

In analogy to static models, free entry requires the absence of pure profits. Thus, the present value v of the future profit stream resulting from the development of a new variety must equal its development costs $c_R(w_L, w_H)/n$ which can be derived from the corresponding production function. Thus, the free-entry condition yields

$$v = c_R(w_L, w_H)/n, \tag{9}$$

with the present value v defined as

$$v(t) = \int_t^\infty \exp[-(R(\tau) - R(t))]\pi(\tau)d\tau, \tag{10}$$

where profits $\pi(\tau)$ are discounted by a cumulative factor $R(u) = \int_0^u r(s)ds$ depending on the interest rates $r(s)$.

Consumption side

The consumption side can be treated very briefly. Since the economy is small with respect to the rest of the world, agents can buy and sell any quantities they judge as optimal at world market prices. Thus, we do not have to worry about demand functions for X and Z. What we have to take into consideration, however, is how consumers in the home economy allocate expenditure E over time. This is given by (see, e.g., Grossman and Helpman, 1989, p. 1265)

$$\dot{E}/E = r - \rho,$$

where r is the interest rate at time t and ρ is the constant individual time preference rate.

Market equilibria

Let us now turn to the specification of market equilibria. As already mentioned, the adoption of a small open economy framework allows to neglect equilibrium conditions for final goods; therefore only the market for the differentiated intermediate goods and the factor markets have to be taken into account.

In specifying market equilibria for middle goods, which will be expressed in terms of the index D, we use the fact that all varieties are equally priced; this simplifies the expression for the supplied quantity of D (4) to

$$D^S = n^{1/\theta} y^S = n^{(1-\theta)/\theta} Y^S. \tag{11}$$

Thus, equilibrium on the market for middle goods reads (cf. (3))

$$n^{(1-\theta)/\theta}Y^S = \eta\frac{p_X}{p_D}X^S + \eta\frac{p_Z}{p_D}Z^S. \tag{12}$$

The factor market clearing conditions can be obtained by equating aggregated demand of the four sectors to households' inelastic supply of factors,

$$\begin{aligned} a_{LR}(w_L,w_H)g + b_{LY}(w_L,w_H)Y^S + b_{LX}(p_X,w_L)X^S + b_{LZ}(p_Z,w_L)Z^S &= L, \\ a_{HR}(w_L,w_H)g + b_{HY}(w_L,w_H)Y^S + b_{HX}(p_X,w_L)X^S + b_{HZ}(p_Z,w_L)Z^S &= H. \end{aligned} \tag{13}$$

Growth rate, wages and output

The specification of the model as given above implies (cf. appendix) that new intermediate goods are introduced at a rate of

$$g = \eta(1-\theta)\frac{w_L L + w_H H}{c_R(w_L,w_H)} - (1-\eta(1-\theta))\rho, \tag{14}$$

under the assumption of internationally immobile financial capital. Since world market prices are constant and no adjustment costs are included in the model, there are no adjustment dynamics; therefore, immediately after trade opens up, both factor rewards and (therefore linear homogenous) unit costs $c_R(w_L,w_H)$ increase at the rate $\eta((1-\theta)/\theta)g$, implying an increasing per capita income and that g is constant, respectively. Now define composite "productivity-adjusted" (Grossman and Helpman, 1991, p. 150) unit demand functions $a_{ij}(\cdot)$, $i = L,H$, $j = X,Z$, which stand for the total quantity of factors needed for the production of one unit of output (both for assembling the final good and for producing the middle product). Then it can be shown that the factor market clearing condition (13) can be expressed by[5]

$$\begin{aligned} a_{LR}g(\rho) + a_{LX}X + a_{LZ}Z &= L, \\ a_{HR}g(\rho) + a_{HX}X + a_{HZ}Z &= H, \end{aligned} \tag{15}$$

where productivity adjusted unit demand functions $a_{ij}(\cdot)$ and modified output X and Z are constant. X and Z are transformations of X^S and Z^S given by $X := X^S \exp[-\eta((1-\theta)/\theta)g(\rho)t]$ and analogously for Z. This transformation is a technically simplifying step and allows us to undertake comparative statics with ρ, L and H as exogenous variables. It should be borne in mind, however, that the output of both final goods X^S and Z^S grows at the same constant rate of

[5] Since in the following we will stress the importance of the time preference rate, the growth rate is written as $g(\rho)$.

$\eta((1-\theta)/\theta)g(\rho)$, as well as factor rewards do, reflecting the increase of productivity due to technological progress.

So far nothing has been said about the value the growth rate takes or about X and Z. The growth rate is positive, if the country is not too small given its preferences, technology and world market prices. In figure 5.1 the line denoted by $g = 0$ gives the loci which divides the factor endowment space into an area where innovation takes place and one where the growth rate is zero[6]. Parallel to this zero-growth line, which can be found by setting $g = 0$ in equation (14), other iso-growth lines can be drawn. The more the distance between the two lines increases, the higher the growth rate the second line represents. An example of an iso-growth line with positive growth is the line $g = g_1$. The area delimited by the axes and the zero-growth line is characterized by zero growth.

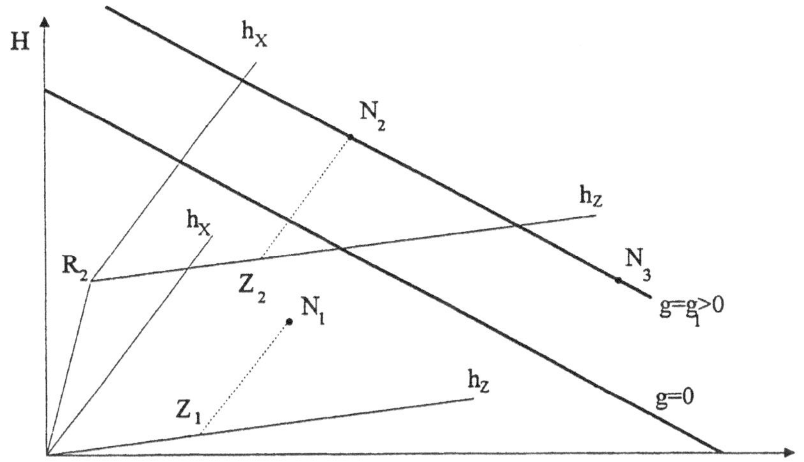

Figure 5.1: Cone of diversification of the small open economy

[6] The growth rate cannot become negative, since this would either require an allocation of a negative quantity of factors to the R&D sector or a reduction of the number of middle goods. Since the former does not make sense and the latter is not possible by definition, growth must always be non-negative.

The conditions for incomplete specialization $(X > 0, Z > 0)$ can be related to the conditions in the traditional Heckscher-Ohlin model: Provided that the factor endowment lies within a certain cone of diversification the country produces both the high-tech good and food. In contrast to other Heckscher-Ohlin models, however, the cone of diversification changes as the growth rate changes, hence a close relationship between the conditions for X and Z to be positive and the growth rate.

Consider an endowment represented by the point N_1. In this case the country's growth rate is zero and the factor market clearing conditions (15) become

$$\begin{bmatrix} a_{LX} & a_{LZ} \\ a_{HX} & a_{HZ} \end{bmatrix} \begin{bmatrix} X \\ Z \end{bmatrix} = \begin{bmatrix} L \\ H \end{bmatrix},$$

just as in a two good, two factor model. Letting $h_j := a_{Hj}/a_{Lj}$, $j = X, Z$ define the human capital intensity of the production processes, the boundaries of this cone of diversification are given by $h_Z L < H < h_X L$. In figure 5.1 the cone is delimited by the lines starting from the origin and denoted by h_Z and h_X.

Now assume that the endowment of the home economy is such that the growth rate is positive; to be concrete, take a point which lies on the line $g = g_1$. Then by equation (14) the value of the growth rate is unambiguously determined and the factors allocated to R&D are given by the vector $(a_{LR}, a_{HR})g(\rho)$ which is depicted in the figure by R_2. Now by rewriting the factor market clearing conditions as

$$\begin{bmatrix} a_{LX} & a_{LZ} \\ a_{HX} & a_{HZ} \end{bmatrix} \begin{bmatrix} X \\ Z \end{bmatrix} = \begin{bmatrix} L - a_{LR}g(\rho) \\ H - a_{HR}g(\rho) \end{bmatrix}, \tag{16}$$

it is obvious that the boundaries of the cone of diversification whose origin lies now at R_2 have the same slopes as the one starting from the origin O. If the endowment point lies inside (e.g. N_2) then the allocation of factors to the manufacturing sectors can be derived in the usual way by drawing a parallel line to h_X starting from N_2; R_2Z_2 is then the quantity of factors allocated to sector Z and Z_2N_2 is the quantity of factors allocated to sector X. If the point lies outside the cone of diversification (e.g. N_3), the country specializes completely in the production of one good (for N_3 in food Z).

Apart from factor endowment, the growth rate is further influenced by world market prices, the time preference rate ρ and the technological parameter η and θ. The impact of prices is ambiguous, we know, however, that g decreases in both θ

and ρ and increases in η. Whereas the interpretation for η and ρ is obvious, the parameter θ deserves further attention: A decrease in θ implies a decrease in the elasticity of substitution $\varepsilon = 1/(1-\theta)$ between two varieties which in turn expresses a higher marginal gain from an additional variety (the derivative of (11) with respect to n decreases in θ). Consequently the lower the elasticity of substitution the higher are prices (cf. (6)) charged by firms producing the intermediate good. Since higher prices go along with higher current profits, the incentive for firms to develop new varieties will be higher, thus the probability of g to be positive is higher.

Since we are interested in a situation where the country produces both goods and grows at a positive rate of g, we assume in the following that the country's endowment is given by a point such as N_2.

3. Factor endowment and trade patterns

In the model presented above, at least two factors can be made out which influence the country's trade pattern: The time preference rate and the factor endowment. Throughout the following analysis it is assumed that they constitute the only difference between the small open economy and its trading partners. This implies that demand functions for final goods are internationally identical which allows to infer trade patterns of an economy from its output.

Whereas factor endowment is probably *the* determinant of trade pattern in the literature, the role of impatience has so far attracted less attention. Before we are going to analyze the impact of factor endowment on trade patterns in this section a remark on (the absence of) Ricardian features of the model: Due to the assumption of limited (i.e. only country wide) dissemination of knowledge, the technology will differ between countries: Take, say, the production function for good Z (neglect constants), insert the expression for the input index given by (11) and insert the production function for Y. One finds $Z = n^{\eta\frac{1-\theta}{\theta}} H^{\alpha+\gamma} L^{2-\eta-\alpha-\gamma}$ which means that the output of Z grows at a rate of $\eta((1-\theta)/\theta)g(\rho)$ if the allocation of factors to this sector is constant. The production function for X can be rewritten analogously as $X = n^{\eta\frac{1-\theta}{\theta}} H^{\beta+\gamma} L^{2-\eta-\beta-\gamma}$. Since the output of X grows at the same rate as the output of Z, the relative productivities at home and abroad are the same[7]. Thus, though the absolute productivity differs between the home economy and the rest of the world (the economies might even overtake each other), Ricardian effects play no role in this setting.

Factor endowment

Let us now discuss trade patterns when the home economy differs from its economic environment only in its factor endowment, i.e. the rate of time preference is assumed to be the same everywhere in the world. If the economy was endowed as indicated by N_1 (cf. figure 5.1), the influence of factor endowment on trade patterns could be studied by standard trade theorems. The Heckscher-Ohlin Theorem would tell us that an increase of the factor endowment ratio H/L leads to an increase of the output ratio X/Z. As a consequence, a shift of N_1 on the line ON_1 (not drawn) would not change the output ratio and thus neither the trade pattern. In economies with positive growth rates (e.g. factor endowment point N_2), however, a relationship between the output ratio and the factor endowment ratio can not be as easily established. Analogy would suggest that moving N_2 on the line R_2N_2 (not drawn) would not change the output ratio. This, however, does not hold since a, say, upward shift implies an increase of the growth rate which in turn requires a higher quantity of factors allocated to R&D. As a consequence, R_2 (and with R_2 the cone of diversification) would shift upwards. Therefore, in order to study the relationship between trade patterns and factor endowment, we first have to find out how the factor endowment has to change such that the output ratio does *not* change.

7 If we had assumed that intermediate goods have an unequal effect on the productivity of factors in the production of the final goods (in our specification the output elasticity of the input index is identical in both production functions), then different growth rates would imply an endogenous change of relative productivity. However, a balanced growth path analysis would then be ruled out (compare Grossman and Helpman, 1991, p. 146).

Figure 5.2 reproduces the factor endowment point in consideration, the origin of its cone of diversification and the iso-growth line it lies on (compare figure 5.1). In addition the factor endowment ratio is drawn as the dotted line ON_2 and an iso-output ratio line ξ_2 is shown which gives the loci where all countries with positive (but different) growth rates and identical output ratio lie on. This line can be found as follows: Solving the factor market clearing conditions (15) for X and Z and dividing results in the output ratio equation[8]

$$\frac{X}{Z} = \frac{g(\rho)a_{LR}a_{LZ}(h_R - h_Z) + a_{HZ}L - a_{LZ}H}{g(\rho)a_{LR}a_{LX}(h_X - h_R) - a_{HX}L + a_{LX}H}.$$

Setting $X/Z = \xi$, inserting the expression for the growth rate (14) and solving for H gives the loci where the output-ratio does not change.

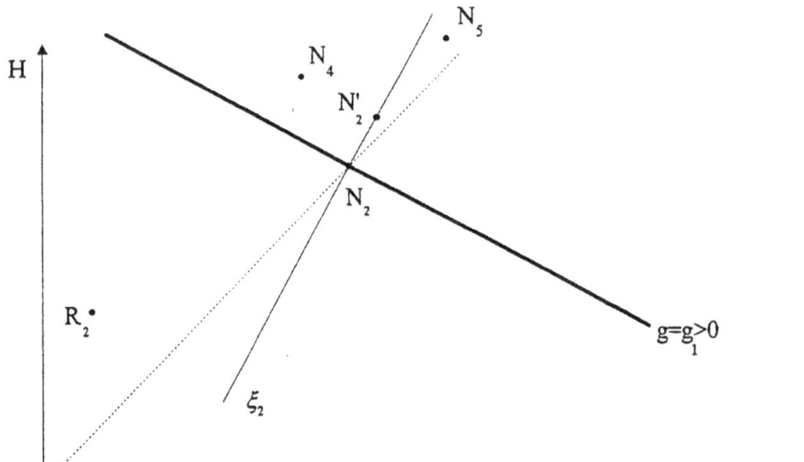

Figure 5.2: Iso-growth and iso-output ratio line

Without going too far into details (cf. appendix) it is worthwhile to mention that the intersection point of this line with the H-axis lies below the origin which is the

8 Remember that constant world market prices p_X and p_Z imply constant factor rewards w_H and w_L, constant unit input factors a_{ij} and constant factor intensities h_j.

reason why it intersects the line R_2N_2 (not drawn) and the endowment ratio line ON_2 from below.

In looking how factors are re-allocated if N_2 shifts upwards, it becomes clear why a shift on R_2N_2 is not enough to keep the output ratio constant: A fraction of the additional factor endowment the economy gets by shifting N_2 will go to the R&D sector which, by assumption, is the most human capital intensive one. Thus, the more the economy shifts on the line R_2N_2, the more the ratio of human capital to labour, provided for the sectors X and Z decreases which excludes a constant output ratio. Therefore, some more human capital must be added in order to keep that ratio constant which then allows to keep the output ratio unchanged. Consequently the slope of the iso-output ratio line must be larger than the slope of the line R_2N_2.

Now consider the following

Lemma

The output ratio X/Z increases, if the factor endowment ratio H/L increases on an iso-growth line, given that the three activities of R&D and manufacturing X and Z can be uniquely ranked by factor intensity h_i such that $h_R > h_X > h_Z$.

$$\left.\frac{\partial(X/Z)}{\partial(H/L)}\right|_{g=const.} > 0 \text{ if } h_R > h_X > h_Z.$$

Proof: An increase of H/L on an iso-growth line requires an increase of H and a simultaneous decrease of L. Since $g(\rho)$ is constant, factor market clearing conditions (15) are better written in the form of (16). By dividing the increase of H/L into two steps with one factor held constant in each step, the application of the Rybczynski theorem completes the proof. ◊

This allows us to complete our investigation of the influence of factor endowment on trade patterns. Assume a country whose endowment is given by N_2 and another country whose endowment is given by N_4. Then the output ratio of country 2 is identical to the output ratio of an (imaginary) country whose endowment is given by N_2' since they share an iso-output line. Country 2', however, can be placed on the same iso-growth line as country 4 and therefore by the above lemma we know that the output ratio of country 4 is higher than the output ratio of country 2. Thus the more a country lies to the left of ξ_2, the higher its output ratio.

Given this situation, it should be obvious why a country relatively abundant in one factor does no longer necessarily export the good making relatively intensive use of this factor, even if countries differ only in their factor endowment. Compare endowment point N_2 and N_5. Prediction by physical factor abundance would state an export of the capital intensive good by country 5 and an import of that good by country 2, because country 5 is physically relatively capital rich. Country 5, however, experiences a higher growth rate which can be achieved only be reducing the human capital abundance of the manufacturing sectors below the one of country 2. Therefore country 2 exports the human capital intensive good and country 5 exports the labour intensive good. This has proven proposition 1:

Proposition 1

A country which is physically capital rich will export the labour intensive good if its human capital intensive R&D sector employs a high share of human capital and thereby leaves a labour rich factor endowment for the production sectors of the economy.

Please note that this implies that countries trade with each other, even if they share a common factor endowment ratio, though there are no differences in the countries apart from the absolute size of factor endowment.

The next section will generalize the result that a physically capital rich country exports the labour intensive good which was shown to hold here for a relatively small part of the factor endowment space. The same result can be obtained if we let interact factor endowment and discount factor as determinants of trade patterns.

4. Time preference, factor endowment and trade patterns

In the last section we discussed trade patterns as determined by factor endowment which is one determinant of the trade pattern of the economy. This determinant adds to the influence time preference rates exert. In the present section, we first exhibit the effect discount factors have on trade patterns (which we will call "impatience-effect") in a world economy in which all determinants of trade patterns other than the difference in the discount factor are ignored. Then we study the interaction of differences in time preference and factor endowment.

Time preference

The "impatience-effect" is demonstrated for the balanced growth path with a positive growth rate of a small open economy with incomplete specialization. In this case the factor market clearing conditions are given by (15). Assume a change of the individual discount factor. The effects are summarized in proposition 2.

Proposition 2

With constant prices and a unique ranking of factor intensities, an increase of the discount factor of the representative consumer leads (a) to a lower growth rate and (b) to a relative increase of the output of the high-tech product. With internationally identical demand functions for final goods (b) is equivalent to saying that the "impatient country" has a tendency to export the human capital intensive good.

(a) $g'(\rho) < 0$,

(b) $\dfrac{\partial(X/Z)}{\partial\rho} > 0 \text{ if } h_R > h_X > h_Z$.

Proof: (cf. appendix)

Figure 5.3 illustrates this proposition. The box *OLNH* represents the given total factor endowment of our small open economy. *OH* equals total human capital and *OL* total labour force. The rays OR_l, R_lX_l and X_lN represent the allocation of factors to R&D, the high-tech sector *X* and the food industry *Z*, respectively, for a country with a low discount rate. If the same country had a higher discount rate (increasing impatience) allocations would change to OR_h, R_hX_h and X_hN. Fewer resources would be allocated to R&D and thus, the growth rate would be lower. The allocation to the production of the high-tech good increases, which leads to an increase of the output ratio X/Z. Note that the human capital intensity of the different activities, which is reflected by the slope of the rays, does not change since it depends solely on exogenously given world market prices.

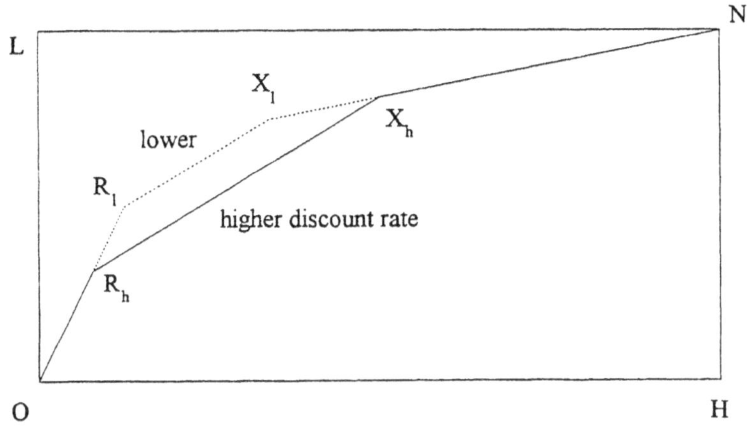

Figure 5.3: The allocation of factors for different time preference rates in a small open economy

The result that the country with a higher (lower) growth rate exports the labour (capital) intensive good could, at first sight, be astonishing. Reformulating the factor market clearing condition and splitting the derivative $\partial(X/Z)/\partial\rho$, however, gives good insight into the economic mechanisms. Write the factor market clearing condition as

$$a_{LX}X + a_{LZ}Z = L - a_{LR}g(\rho),$$
$$a_{HX}X + a_{HZ}Z = H - a_{HR}g(\rho),$$

and split the derivative into

$$\frac{\partial(X/Z)}{\partial\rho} = \frac{\partial(X/Z)}{\partial(H_{XZ}/L_{XZ})}\frac{\partial(H_{XZ}/L_{XZ})}{\partial\rho},$$

where H_{XZ} and L_{XZ} is the total allocation of human capital and labour in the X and the Z sector, respectively $(H_{XZ} = H_X + H_Z, L_{XZ} = L_X + L_Z)$. The first term is the change of the output ratio with respect to the change of the factor endowment after subtracting the factors allocated to R&D. This is the Heckscher-Ohlin theorem. The second derivative gives the change of the factor endowments available for the manufacturing activities with respect to a change of the discount rate. Both derivatives are positive if $h_R > h_X > h_Z$.

This splitting of the derivative allows to give an economic interpretation: An increase of the discount factor, by reducing the R&D activity (implying a lower growth rate), increases the factor endowment ratio of the rest of the economy, which is due to the fact that the R&D sector is (by assumption) the most human capital intensive one. The rest of the economy then produces relatively more of the high-tech product than before. Obviously, this implies that two countries which differ in their time preference rate (cf. figure 5.3) and take world market prices as given (assume they are both small) will trade with each other though they have identical endowment. In contrast to static models, where trade between countries with identical endowment trade requires internationally different demand functions for final goods, the result here is solely due to differences in the time preference rate.

Interaction of time preference rate and factor endowment

We are now in the position to study the interaction between the determinants of trade patterns. Assume an economy (cf. figure 5.1) endowed with human capital and labour as given by N_2 and whose time preference rate ρ increases. This shifts the zero-growth line to the right which decreases the distance to the line $g = g_1$. Thus the growth rate g_1, with factor endowments unchanged, falls, which implies a decrease of the quantity of factors allocated to R&D and a shift of R_2 towards the origin. Consequently the vector Z_2N_2, reflecting the factors used in sector X, increases whereas at the same time the length of the vector R_2Z_2 decreases. Now change the factor endowment ratio by moving the endowment point N_2 (for simplicity on the iso-growth line) towards N_3. Clearly, this has the opposite effect with respect to the output ratio X/Z. The trade pattern which will finally result therefore depends on which effect is more important compared to the factor endowment and discount rate of the trading partner. We can easily imagine, however, that the "impatience-effect" becomes stronger than the factor endowment effect and thus a physically relatively capital rich country becomes an importer of the capital intensive good and an exporter of the labour intensive good.

5. The price version of the Heckscher-Ohlin theorem

The ambiguity concerning trade patterns and physical factor richness due to different growth rates leads to a failure of the quantity version of the Heckscher-Ohlin theorem. We will now show that all of these findings can be nicely integrated in the pure theory of international trade by evoking, as trade theorists might already have conjectured, a price-version of the Heckscher-Ohlin theorem (cf. e.g. Ethier, 1984, p. 141).

First consider economies with identical discount rates which differ only in their factor endowment. In two good, two factor "traditional" Heckscher-Ohlin models a shift of an economy's endowment which does not change the economy's capital to labour ratio does not change its output ratio. Expressing factor abundance in terms of autarky factor-price ratio ω also yields that a shift of the factor endowment point of the economy which does not change the economy's capital to labour ratio does not change ω. Thus a shift on the output ratio conserving line is equivalent to keeping the autarky price ratio constant. Drawing an analogy to the model presented here[9] a shift on the output ratio conserving line ξ_2 in figure 5.2 implies a constant autarky wage ratio $\omega := w_H/w_L$. It can easily be shown that an increase of H (and a decrease of L) decreases ω, hence a decrease of the factor endowment ratio parallel to the L-axis leads to higher ω. Therefore shifting N_2 on the line ξ_2 does not change ω; shifting it further to N_5 increases the autarky wage ratio, and consequently, under free trade country 5 exports the labour intensive good and country 2 imports it.

Now consider two countries which differ only in their discount factors. In order to predict trade patterns in a correct way, ω must fall in ρ. In fact, we can show:

Proposition 3

In autarky the country with higher patience (lower time preference rate) has a higher factor reward ratio w_H/w_L and thus is economically human capital poor. Consequently, under free trade, it will export the labour intensive good:

$$\frac{\partial(w_H/w_L)}{\partial \rho} < 0 \text{ if } h_R > h_x > h_Z.$$

[9] Unfortunately, we have so far been unable to proof this formally.

Proof: (cf. appendix)

This result has an easy economic interpretation. If ρ decreases, the consumers' preferences shift from consumption today to consumption in the future which induces increased R&D. Since the R&D sector is the most human capital intensive one, human capital becomes relatively more scarce, and thus, the wage ratio increases.

Finally consider the interaction of factor endowment and discount factor. In the last section the measure for capital richness was the physical endowment ratio H/L. H/L reflects only partially the determinants of the output ratio $\xi = X/Z$ which depends on the time preference rate and the endowment of human capital and labour: $\xi = \xi(\rho, H, L)$. Thus it is not enough to know the ratio of production factors in order to predict trade patterns. Moreover, it is in any case possible to "cheat" by choosing an appropriate ρ. In contrast to the physical endowment ratio, the autarky factor reward ratio w_H/w_L itself is a function of all factors which influence the output ratio: $\omega = \omega(\rho, H, L)$. Since it decreases in ρ and it behaves in the same way as the output ratio with respect to factor endowment (as was shown by analogous reasoning above), it can be used as a correct predictor of trade patterns.

6. Conclusion

In a small open economy model of endogenous growth we have shown that in contrast to standard trade theory results, the production structure of an economy does not depend on its relative factor endowment but on its absolute size, measured in physical factor endowment. The basic engine of growth is a domestic public stock of knowledge which is used by and a by-product of the R&D sector. Due to the absence of (or imperfect) international flows of knowledge a larger economy will experience a higher rate of growth. Higher growth rates require a higher allocation of factors in the R&D sector which by assumption uses human capital most intensively. Thus, more human capital than labour is withdrawn from the manufacturing part of the economy which will therefore be left with a lower human capital to labour ratio. In a trade perspective this means that an economy with a higher growth rate has a tendency to specialize in the production of the labour intensive good. Comparing factor endowment ratios alone does therefore no longer form a solid basis for predicting trade patterns. In a world where factor endowments are the only determinant of trade patterns, a physically capital rich country can therefore easily become an exporter of the labour intensive good.

Taking the time preference rate into consideration, we found that it influences trade patterns by its effect on the growth rate, too. The more impatient a country, the lower its growth rate; less factors are employed in the R&D sector and the trading sectors have a more human capital rich endowment at their disposal. Thus, a country with a high time preference rate has a tendency to export the human capital intensive good. As a corollary one finds that two countries with identical factor endowment and identical demand function for final goods will trade with each other in final goods if their time preference rates differ.

Combining the impatience effect and the factor endowment effect can again lead to a failure of the quantity version of the Heckscher-Ohlin theorem and make a physically capital rich country an exporter of the labour intensive good if the mechanism factor endowment and time preference rates exert on the growth rate makes the production sectors relatively labour rich.

Given this result, at first sight contradictory to standard theorems of the pure theory of international trade, we have finally shown that the price version of the Heckscher-Ohlin theorem, where factor richness is measured in terms of autarky factor rewards, can indeed explain the outcome. The higher the growth rate of an economy the higher relative demand by the R&D sector for human capital and the higher the autarky factor reward ratio $\omega := w_H / w_L$ since this factor is most intensively used in the R&D process. Thus, in contrast to the quantity version of the Heckscher-Ohlin theorem, the price version does correctly predict trade patterns.

One assumption of the model deserves further attention: Since knowledge was assumed to disseminate only locally, growth rates can differ between countries which is one stylized fact required for growth models. In this respect the model is in line with Feenstra (1990) or Grossman and Helpman (1991, ch. 9.3). This assumption allows to model endogenously the fact that some countries' consumption per capita rises faster as other countries' does and might even overtake. Another empirical finding, the change of trade patterns as observed e.g. for the Japanese economy by Balassa and Noland (1989) or Grossman (1990), can be found in this model only by an exogenous change of the individual time preference rate. An extension of this model to a two-country world in the next chapter allows by including human capital accumulation to analyze endogenous changes of trade patterns.

Appendix

1. Unit cost functions

We derive unit cost functions for a general, n-factor Cobb-Douglas production function with constant returns to scale. The three factor case in the main text then follows directly. The unit production function reads

$$1 = Ax_1^{\alpha_1}x_2^{\alpha_2}\cdots x_n^{\alpha_n} = A\prod_{i=1}^{n} x_i^{\alpha_i}, \quad \sum_{i=1}^{n}\alpha_i = 1,$$

where x_i is the quantity of factor i employed for production, α_i are the output elasticities and A is a constant. The problem of an optimal choice of inputs consists in $\min_{x_i} \sum_{i=1}^{n} w_i x_i$ subject to the unit production function. The Lagrangian reads

$$\mathcal{L} = \sum_{i=1}^{n} w_i x_i - \lambda\left(A\prod_{i=1}^{n} x_i^{\alpha_i} - 1\right)$$

and the first order conditions are

$$w_i = \lambda A\left(\prod_{i=1}^{n} x_i^{\alpha_i}\right)\frac{\alpha_i x_i^{\alpha_i - 1}}{x_i^{\alpha_i}} = \lambda\alpha_i x_i^{-1} \Leftrightarrow x_i = \lambda\alpha_i w_i^{-1}$$

and the unit production function. Combine the first order conditions to obtain

$$A\prod_{i=1}^{n}\left(\lambda\alpha_i w_i^{-1}\right)^{\alpha_i} = A\lambda\prod_{i=1}^{n}\left(\alpha_i w_i^{-1}\right)^{\alpha_i} = 1.$$

Choosing the constant A such that $A=\prod_{i=1}^{n}(\alpha_i)^{-\alpha_i}$ this is equivalent to $\lambda=\prod_{i=1}^{n} w_i^{\alpha_i}$. Reinserting into the first first order condition gives $x_i=\left(\prod_{i=1}^{n} w_i^{\alpha_i}\right)\alpha_i w_i^{-1}$, which finally leads to the unit cost function

$$c=\sum_{j=1}^{n} w_j x_j=\sum_{j=1}^{n} w_j\left(\prod_{i=1}^{n} w_i^{\alpha_i}\right)\alpha_j w_j^{-1}=\prod_{i=1}^{n} w_i^{\alpha_i}.$$

2. Demand for the differentiated good: Deriving equation (11)

We derive demand and unit cost functions resulting from an production function as given in (10). In contrast to the main text, varieties are indexed by i.

Demand function

$$\min_{y^i}=\int_0^n p_y^i y^i di \text{ subject to } \left(\int_0^n (y^i)^\theta di\right)^{1/\theta}=D^S.$$

The Lagrange function is

$$\mathcal{L}=\int_0^n p_y^i y^i di+\lambda\left(D^S-\left(\int_0^n (y^i)^\theta di\right)^{1/\theta}\right).$$

The first order conditions read

$$\mathcal{L}_{y^i}=p_y^i-\lambda\frac{1}{\theta}\left(\int_0^n (y^i)^\theta di\right)^{\frac{1}{\theta}-1}\theta(y^i)^{\theta-1}=0,$$

$$\mathcal{L}_\lambda=D^S-\left(\int_0^n (y^i)^\theta di\right)^{1/\theta}=0.$$

The first condition can be rearranged,

$$p_y^i=\lambda\frac{1}{\theta}\left(\int_0^n (y^i)^\theta di\right)^{\frac{1-\theta}{\theta}}\theta(y^i)^{\theta-1}\Leftrightarrow(p_y^i)^{\frac{\theta}{1-\theta}}(y^i)^\theta=\lambda^{\frac{\theta}{1-\theta}}\int_0^n (y^i)^\theta di.$$

Now write the second condition as (again, as in the appendix of chapter 2, this is possible since the RHS of the last equation does not depend on di)

$$D^S=\left(\int_0^n \frac{(p_y^i)^{\frac{\theta}{1-\theta}}(y^i)^\theta}{(p_y^i)^{\frac{\theta}{1-\theta}}(y^i)^\theta}(y^i)^\theta di\right)^{1/\theta}=\left((p_y^i)^{\frac{\theta}{1-\theta}}(y^i)^\theta\int_0^n (p_y^i)^{\frac{-\theta}{1-\theta}}di\right)^{1/\theta}.$$

Solve this and find

$$y^i = \frac{\left(p_y^i\right)^{-\frac{1}{1-\theta}}}{\left(\int_0^n \left(p_y^i\right)^{-\frac{\theta}{1-\theta}} di\right)^{1/\theta}} D^S = \frac{\left(p_y^i\right)^{-\varepsilon}}{\left(\int_0^n \left(p_y^i\right)^{1-\varepsilon} di\right)^{\frac{\varepsilon}{\varepsilon-1}}} D^S,$$

where $\varepsilon = 1/(1-\theta)$. If all goods are equally priced, we have

$$y^i = \frac{\left(p_y^i\right)^{-\varepsilon}}{\left(n\left(p_y^i\right)^{1-\varepsilon}\right)^{\frac{\varepsilon}{\varepsilon-1}}} D^S = \frac{D^S}{n^{\frac{\varepsilon}{\varepsilon-1}}} = \frac{D^S}{n^{\frac{1}{\theta}}}.$$

Unit cost function

The unit cost function can now be easily derived by inserting the factor demand function into the total cost function. This gives

$$C = \int_0^n p_y^i y^i di = \int_0^n p_y^i \frac{\left(p_y^i\right)^{-\frac{1}{1-\theta}}}{\left(\int_0^n \left(p_y^i\right)^{-\frac{\theta}{1-\theta}} di\right)^{1/\theta}} D^S di =$$

$$= \left(\int_0^n \left(p_y^i\right)^{-\frac{\theta}{1-\theta}} di\right)^{-\frac{1}{\theta}} \int_0^n \left(p_y^i\right)^{-\frac{\theta}{1-\theta}} di\, D^S = \left(\int_0^n \left(p_y^i\right)^{-\frac{\theta}{1-\theta}} di\right)^{1-\frac{1}{\theta}} D^S.$$

Dividing by output D^S and with $\varepsilon = 1/(1-\theta)$ this gives unit cost functions

$$c\left(p_y^i\right) = \left(\int_0^n \left(p_y^i\right)^{-\frac{\theta}{1-\theta}} di\right)^{\frac{\theta-1}{\theta}} = \left(\int_0^n \left(p_y^i\right)^{1-\varepsilon} di\right)^{\frac{1}{1-\varepsilon}}.$$

3. Solution of the model

The solution is largely inspired by Grossman and Helpman (1991a, ch. 6).

3.1. Factor rewards

Here we determine the relationship between factor prices and exogenously given world market goods prices. Free trade imposes world market prices for the freely traded final goods; thus unit costs must satisfy

$$p_Z = c_Z(\cdot) = w_H^{\alpha} p_D^{\eta} w_L^{1-\eta-\alpha},$$

$$p_X = c_X(\cdot) = w_H^{\beta} p_D^{\eta} w_L^{1-\eta-\beta}.$$

Since we know that all intermediates are equally priced, the expression for the price of the input index simplifies to

$$p_D = \left(\int_0^n (p_y)^{1-\varepsilon} di\right)^{1/(1-\varepsilon)} = n^{1/(1-\varepsilon)} p_y = n^{-(1-\theta)/\theta} p_y. \tag{A.1}$$

With equation (12) the pricing equations are equivalent to

$$p_Z = w_H^{\alpha} \left(n^{-\frac{1-\theta}{\theta}} \frac{w_H^{\gamma} w_L^{1-\gamma}}{\theta} \right)^{\eta} w_L^{1-\eta-\alpha},$$

$$p_X = w_H^{\beta} \left(n^{-\frac{1-\theta}{\theta}} \frac{w_H^{\gamma} w_L^{1-\gamma}}{\theta} \right)^{\eta} w_L^{1-\eta-\beta}.$$

Rearranging yields

$$w_H^{\alpha+\gamma\eta} w_L^{1-\eta\gamma-\alpha} = p_Z n^{\eta\frac{1-\theta}{\theta}} \theta^{\eta},$$

$$w_H^{\beta+\gamma\eta} w_L^{1-\eta\gamma-\beta} = p_X n^{\eta\frac{1-\theta}{\theta}} \theta^{\eta}.$$

Since commodity prices are fixed by world markets, taking logarithms and deriving with respect to time results in

$$(\alpha+\gamma\eta)\frac{\dot{w}_H}{w_H} + (1-\eta\gamma-\alpha)\frac{\dot{w}_L}{w_L} = \eta\frac{1-\theta}{\theta}\frac{\dot{n}}{n},$$

$$(\beta+\gamma\eta)\frac{\dot{w}_H}{w_H} + (1-\eta\gamma-\beta)\frac{\dot{w}_L}{w_L} = \eta\frac{1-\theta}{\theta}\frac{\dot{n}}{n}.$$

This can be solved for the growth rates of factor rewards as a function of the innovation rate $g := \dot{n}/n$. The determinant is

$$Det = (\alpha+\gamma\eta)(1-\eta\gamma-\beta) - (\beta+\gamma\eta)(1-\eta\gamma-\alpha) =$$

$$= \alpha - \alpha\eta\gamma - \alpha\beta + \gamma\eta - (\gamma\eta)^2 - \beta\gamma\eta - \left(\beta - \beta\eta\gamma - \alpha\beta + \gamma\eta - (\gamma\eta)^2 - \alpha\gamma\eta\right) =$$

$$= \alpha - \beta < 0.$$

and the growth rate of factor rewards is

$$\frac{\dot{w}_H}{w_H} = \frac{\eta\frac{1-\theta}{\theta} g(\alpha-\beta)}{D} = \eta\frac{1-\theta}{\theta} g,$$

$$\frac{\dot{w}_L}{w_L} = \frac{(\alpha-\beta)\eta\frac{1-\theta}{\theta} g}{D} = \eta\frac{1-\theta}{\theta} g.$$

Thus as long as world market prices are fixed and new intermediate goods are introduced at the rate g, both factor rewards grow at the rate $\eta\left((1-\theta)/\theta\right)g$, reflecting the increase of the productivity of factors due to technological progress.

3.2. Factor market clearing conditions

Here the full derivation of (21) is given. We start from (19) which is reproduced here for convenience.

$$\begin{aligned} &a_{LR}(w_L,w_H)g+b_{LY}(w_L,w_H)Y^S+b_{LX}(p_X,w_L)X^S+b_{LZ}(p_Z,w_L)Z^S=L,\\ &a_{HR}(w_L,w_H)g+b_{HY}(w_L,w_H)Y^S+b_{HX}(p_X,w_L)X^S+b_{HZ}(p_Z,w_L)Z^S=H. \end{aligned} \quad (A.2)$$

Using the middle goods market clearing condition (18) factor market clearing conditions can be expressed as

$$a_{LR}(\cdot)g+b_{LY}(\cdot)\left(\frac{\eta}{n^{(1-\theta)/\theta}}\frac{p_X}{p_D}X^S+\frac{\eta}{n^{(1-\theta)/\theta}}\frac{p_Z}{p_D}Z^S\right)+b_{LX}(\cdot)X^S+b_{LZ}(\cdot)Z^S=L,$$

$$a_{HR}(\cdot)g+b_{HY}(\cdot)\left(\frac{\eta}{n^{(1-\theta)/\theta}}\frac{p_X}{p_D}X^S+\frac{\eta}{n^{(1-\theta)/\theta}}\frac{p_Z}{p_D}Z^S\right)+b_{HX}(\cdot)X^S+b_{HZ}(\cdot)Z^S=H.$$

Note that $(\cdot)$ is used for abbreviating notation and does *not* stand for identical arguments. Rearranging yields

$$a_{LR}(\cdot)g+\left(b_{LY}(\cdot)\frac{\eta}{n^{(1-\theta)/\theta}}\frac{p_X}{p_D}+b_{LX}(\cdot)\right)X^S+\left(b_{LY}(\cdot)\frac{\eta}{n^{(1-\theta)/\theta}}\frac{p_Z}{p_D}+b_{LZ}(\cdot)\right)Z^S=L \quad ,(A.3)$$

$$a_{HR}(\cdot)g+\left(b_{HY}(\cdot)\frac{\eta}{n^{(1-\theta)/\theta}}\frac{p_X}{p_D}+b_{HX}(\cdot)\right)X^S+\left(b_{HY}(\cdot)\frac{\eta}{n^{(1-\theta)/\theta}}\frac{p_Z}{p_D}+b_{HZ}(\cdot)\right)Z^S=H.$$

With unit demand functions and equation (A.1) this becomes

$$a_{LR}(\cdot)g+\left(b_{LY}(\cdot)\frac{\eta p_X}{p_y}+(1-\eta-\beta)\frac{p_X}{w_L}\right)X^S+\left(b_{LY}(\cdot)\frac{\eta p_Z}{p_y}+(1-\eta-\alpha)\frac{p_Z}{w_L}\right)Z^S=L,$$

$$a_{HR}(\cdot)g+\left(b_{HY}(\cdot)\frac{\eta p_X}{p_y}+\beta\frac{p_X}{w_H}\right)X^S+\left(b_{HY}(\cdot)\frac{\eta p_Z}{p_y}+\alpha\frac{p_Z}{w_H}\right)Z^S=H. \quad (A.4)$$

We have shown in the last subsection that the imposition of constant goods prices implies a growth rate for factor rewards of $\eta((1-\theta)/\theta)g$. By the linear homogeneity of the price for each variety in factor rewards (cf. (12)), p_y increases at $\eta((1-\theta)/\theta)g$, too.

We now define productivity adjusted gross input coefficients according to (t stands for time):

$$a_{LX}:=\left(b_{LY}(\cdot)\frac{\eta p_X}{p_y}+(1-\eta-\beta)\frac{p_X}{w_L}\right)\exp\left[\eta\frac{1-\theta}{\theta}gt\right],$$

$$a_{HX}:=\left(b_{HY}(\cdot)\frac{\eta p_X}{p_y}+\beta\frac{p_X}{w_H}\right)\exp\left[\eta\frac{1-\theta}{\theta}gt\right], \quad (A.5)$$

$$a_{LZ} := \left(b_{LY}(\cdot)\frac{\eta p_Z}{p_y} + (1-\eta-\alpha)\frac{p_Z}{w_L} \right) \exp\left[\eta \frac{1-\theta}{\theta} gt \right],$$

$$a_{HZ} := \left(b_{HY}(\cdot)\frac{\eta p_Z}{p_y} + \alpha\frac{p_Z}{w_H} \right) \exp\left[\eta \frac{1-\theta}{\theta} gt \right],$$

$$X := X^S \exp\left[-\eta \frac{1-\theta}{\theta} gt \right] \qquad Z := Z^S \exp\left[-\eta \frac{1-\theta}{\theta} gt \right].$$

With these definitions, the factor market clearing conditions can be expressed as

$$a_{LR} g(\rho) + a_{LX} X + a_{LZ} Z = L,$$
$$a_{HR} g(\rho) + a_{HX} X + a_{HZ} Z = H. \tag{A.6}$$

where all unit input functions, the growth rate and (transformed) output are constant as long as world market prices do not change over time.

3.3. Growth rate

So far everything has been expressed as a function of g. But how can the growth rate g be determined? Differentiate (16) with respect to time to obtain $\pi + \dot{v} = rv$. Profits of a representative firm in sector Y can be computed with (17) and (9) as

$$\pi = p_y y - c_y(\cdot) y = (1-\theta) p_y y = (1-\theta) p_y \frac{D^D}{n^{1/\theta}} =$$
$$= (1-\theta) p_y \frac{(\eta p_X / p_D) X^S + (\eta p_Z / p_D) Z^S}{n^{1/\theta}} = (1-\theta)\eta \frac{p_y}{p_D n^{1/\theta}} (p_X X^S + p_Z Z^S).$$

With (A.1) this becomes

$$\pi = (1-\theta)\eta \frac{p_X X^S + p_Z Z^S}{n}.$$

Thus

$$\frac{\dot{v}}{v} = r - \frac{\pi}{v} = r - (1-\theta)\eta \frac{p_X X^S + p_Z Z^S}{nv} = r - (1-\theta)\eta \frac{p_X X^S + p_Z Z^S}{c_R(w_L, w_H)}. \tag{A.7}$$

Since we exclude international financial capital flows, we can express equilibrium of the trade balance as

$$E = p_X X^S + p_Z Z^S, \tag{A.8}$$

which implies, since $\dot{p}_X = \dot{p}_Z = 0$ and X^S and Z^S grow by (A.4) (cf. also (A.5)), that total expenditure grows over time at the rate of $\eta \frac{1-\theta}{\theta} g$. Thus interest rates are given by, since $\dot{E}/E = r - \rho$,

$$r-\rho=\eta\frac{1-\theta}{\theta}g. \tag{A.9}$$

Finally differentiating (15) with respect to time gives

$$\frac{\dot{v}}{v}+\frac{\dot{n}}{n}=\frac{\dot{c}_R(w_L,w_H)}{c_R(w_L,w_H)}=\eta\frac{1-\theta}{\theta}g,$$

which can be expressed as (remember that $g\equiv\dot{n}/n$)

$$\frac{\dot{v}}{v}=\left(\eta\frac{1-\theta}{\theta}-1\right)g. \tag{A.10}$$

The last four numbered equations can be combined to give an explicit function of the growth rate: Insert (A.8) and (A.9) into (A.7), by that eliminate r and obtain

$$\frac{\dot{v}}{v}=\eta\frac{1-\theta}{\theta}g+\rho-(1-\theta)\eta\frac{E}{c_R(w_L,w_H)},$$

With (A.10) this gives

$$g=(1-\theta)\eta\frac{E}{c_R(w_L,w_H)}-\rho. \tag{A.11}$$

Total expenditure E, however, depends on the growth rate g, i.e. in addition to (A.11) we need a second relation between E and g, in order to derive g as a function of "fundamentals" of the model. This second relationship is found with the help of the factor market clearing conditions. Starting from slightly rearranged (A.4)

$$a_{LR}(\cdot)g+\left(b_{LY}(\cdot)\frac{\eta}{p_y}+\frac{1-\eta-\beta}{w_L}\right)p_X X^S+\left(b_{LY}(\cdot)\frac{\eta}{p_y}+\frac{1-\eta-\alpha}{w_L}\right)p_Z Z^S=L,$$

$$a_{HR}(\cdot)g+\left(b_{HY}(\cdot)\frac{\eta}{p_y}+\frac{\beta}{w_H}\right)p_X X^S+\left(b_{HY}(\cdot)\frac{\eta}{p_y}+\frac{\alpha}{w_H}\right)p_Z Z^S=H.$$

we multiply the equations by w_L and w_H, respectively and sum up:

$$\left(w_L a_{LR}(\cdot)+w_H a_{HR}(\cdot)\right)g+\left(w_L b_{LY}(\cdot)\frac{\eta}{p_y}+1-\eta+w_H b_{HY}(\cdot)\frac{\eta}{p_y}\right)p_X X^S+$$

$$+\left(w_L b_{LY}(\cdot)\frac{\eta}{p_y}+1-\eta+w_H b_{HY}(\cdot)\frac{\eta}{p_y}\right)p_Z Z^S=w_L L+w_H H.$$

Inserting explicit expressions for b_{LY} and b_{HY} and using equations (12) and (A.8) we find

$$\left(w_L a_{LR}(\cdot)+w_H a_{HR}(\cdot)\right)g+\left(1-\eta(1-\theta)\right)E=w_L L+w_H H, \tag{A.12}$$

which is the second equation required.

The determinant for the equation system (A.11) and (A.12) is given by

$$D=-\left(w_L a_{LR}(\cdot)+w_H a_{HR}(\cdot)\right)\frac{(1-\theta)\eta}{c_R(w_L,w_H)}-\left(1-\eta(1-\theta)\right)=$$
$$=-(1-\theta)\eta-\left(1-\eta(1-\theta)\right)=-1.$$

Thus the solutions for g and E are

$$g=(w_L L+w_H H)\frac{(1-\theta)\eta}{c_R(w_L,w_H)}-\rho\left(1-\eta(1-\theta)\right)=\eta(1-\theta)\frac{w_L L+w_H H}{c_R(w_L,w_H)}-\left(1-\eta(1-\theta)\right)\rho,$$
$$E=\left(w_L a_{LR}(\cdot)+w_H a_{HR}(\cdot)\right)\rho+w_L L+w_H H=w_L\left(a_{LR}(\cdot)\rho+L\right)+w_H\left(a_{HR}(\cdot)\rho+H\right).$$

For further calculations we express the growth rate as $g(\rho)=c_1 L+c_2 H-c_3$, where

$$c_1=\eta(1-\theta)\frac{w_L}{c_R(w_L,w_H)},\ c_2=\eta(1-\theta)\frac{w_H}{c_R(w_L,w_H)} \text{ and } c_3=\left(1-\eta(1-\theta)\right)\rho.$$

We note further that with

$$c_R=w_H^{\gamma}w_L^{1-\gamma},\ a_{LR}=(1-\gamma)(w_H/w_L)^{\gamma} \text{ and } a_{HR}=\gamma(w_L/w_H)^{1-\gamma},$$

the positive constants can be rewritten as $c_1=\eta(1-\theta)\frac{1-\gamma}{a_{LR}}$ and $c_2=\eta(1-\theta)\frac{\gamma}{a_{HR}}$.

3.4. Factor intensity of production

Here we give conditions for the exponents of the production functions (1) and (2), under which sector X is always more human capital intensive than sector Z.

The unit demand functions (A.5) can be further simplified by inserting explicit expressions for $b_{LY}(\cdot)$, $b_{HY}(\cdot)$ and p_y. This gives

$$a_{LX}:=\left((1-\gamma)\eta\theta+1-\eta-\beta\right)\frac{p_X}{w_L}\exp\left[\eta\frac{1-\theta}{\theta}gt\right],$$
$$a_{HX}:=\left(\gamma\eta\theta+\beta\right)\frac{p_X}{w_H}\exp\left[\eta\frac{1-\theta}{\theta}gt\right],$$
$$a_{LZ}:=\left((1-\gamma)\eta\theta+1-\eta-\alpha\right)\frac{p_Z}{w_L}\exp\left[\eta\frac{1-\theta}{\theta}gt\right],$$
$$a_{HZ}:=\left(\gamma\eta\theta+\alpha\right)\frac{p_Z}{w_H}\exp\left[\eta\frac{1-\theta}{\theta}gt\right],$$

Let $h_j:=a_{Hj}/a_{Lj}$, $j=R,X,Z$ define the human capital intensity. Then

$$h_X>h_Z\Leftrightarrow\frac{a_{HX}}{a_{LX}}=\frac{\gamma\eta\theta+\beta}{\left((1-\gamma)\eta\theta+1-\eta-\beta\right)}\frac{w_L}{w_H}>\frac{a_{HZ}}{a_{LZ}}=\frac{\gamma\eta\theta+\alpha}{\left((1-\gamma)\eta\theta+1-\eta-\alpha\right)}\frac{w_L}{w_H}.$$

With $c_1 := (1-\gamma)\eta\theta + 1 - \eta > 0$ and $c_2 := \gamma\eta\theta > 0$, this condition becomes $\frac{c_2+\beta}{c_1-\beta} > \frac{c_2+\alpha}{c_1-\alpha}$ which can be rewritten as $(c_2+\beta)(c_1-\alpha) > (c_2+\alpha)(c_1-\beta)$ since both denominators are positive. We can then further deduce

$c_2c_1 + \beta c_1 - c_2\alpha - \beta\alpha > c_2c_1 + \alpha c_1 - c_2\beta - \alpha\beta \Leftrightarrow c_2(\beta-\alpha) > -c_1(\beta-\alpha)$.

Since both constants are positive, this condition can only be satisfied if $\beta > \alpha$.

4. Marginal gains of a new variety

The marginal gain MG of an additional variety is given by

$MG := \frac{\partial D^S}{\partial n} = \frac{1}{\theta} n^{(1-\theta)/\theta} y^S$. Transform monotonically to

$\ln(MG) = \ln\left(\frac{1}{\theta}\right) + \frac{1-\theta}{\theta}\ln(n) + \ln(y^S)$. MG decreases with increasing θ since

$$\frac{\partial \ln(MG)}{\partial\theta} = \frac{1}{1/\theta}\left(-\frac{1}{\theta^2}\right) + \frac{-\theta-(1-\theta)}{\theta^2}\ln(n) = -\frac{1}{\theta} - \frac{1}{\theta^2}\ln(n) < 0.$$

5. Output ratio

The factor market clearing conditions (21) can be written as

$$\begin{bmatrix} a_{LX} & a_{LZ} \\ a_{HX} & a_{HZ} \end{bmatrix}\begin{bmatrix} X \\ Z \end{bmatrix} = \begin{bmatrix} L - a_{LR}g(\rho) \\ H - a_{HR}g(\rho) \end{bmatrix}.$$

The determinant $D = a_{LX}a_{HZ} - a_{HX}a_{LZ} = a_{LX}a_{LZ}(h_Z - h_X) < 0$ is negative due to the assumption on factor intensities. Solving for X and Z we find

$$X = \frac{(L - a_{LR}g(\rho))a_{HZ} - (H - a_{HR}g(\rho))a_{LZ}}{D},$$

$$Z = \frac{a_{LX}(H - a_{HR}g(\rho)) - a_{HX}(L - a_{LR}g(\rho))}{D}.$$

Dividing gives

$$\frac{X}{Z} = \frac{(L - a_{LR}g(\rho))a_{HZ} - (H - a_{HR}g(\rho))a_{LZ}}{a_{LX}(H - a_{HR}g(\rho)) - a_{HX}(L - a_{LR}g(\rho))}. \quad \text{(A.13)}$$

After some rearrangement we find

$$\frac{X}{Z}=\frac{a_{HZ}L-a_{LR}a_{HZ}g(\rho)-a_{LZ}H+a_{HR}a_{LZ}g(\rho)}{a_{LX}H-a_{HR}a_{LX}g(\rho)-a_{HX}L+a_{LR}a_{HX}g(\rho)}.$$

This is equivalent to the expression

$$\frac{X}{Z}=\frac{g(\rho)a_1+a_{HZ}L-a_{LZ}H}{g(\rho)a_2-a_{HX}L+a_{LX}H},$$

where $a_1=a_{HR}a_{LZ}-a_{LR}a_{HZ}=a_{LR}a_{LZ}(h_R-h_Z)>0,$

$a_2=a_{LR}a_{HX}-a_{HR}a_{LX}=a_{LR}a_{LX}(h_X-h_R)<0.$

6. Iso-output ratio line

The output ratio is given by

$$\frac{X}{Z}=\frac{g(\rho)a_1+a_{HZ}L-a_{LZ}H}{g(\rho)a_2-a_{HX}L+a_{LX}H},$$

where $a_1=a_{HR}a_{LZ}-a_{LR}a_{HZ}$, $a_2=a_{LR}a_{HX}-a_{HR}a_{LX}$.

Setting $\xi=X/Z$ the iso-output lines are given by

$$g(\rho)a_2\xi-a_{HX}L\xi+a_{LX}H\xi=g(\rho)a_1+a_{HZ}L-a_{LZ}H \Leftrightarrow$$

$$g(\rho)(a_2\xi-a_1)-L(a_{HX}\xi+a_{HZ})+H(a_{LX}\xi+a_{LZ})=0.$$

Inserting $g=c_1L+c_2H-c_3$, where

$c_1=\eta(1-\theta)\frac{1-\delta}{a_{LR}}$, $c_2=\eta(1-\theta)\frac{\delta}{a_{HR}}$ and $c_3=(1-\eta(1-\theta))\rho$, this becomes

$$c_1L(a_2\xi-a_1)+c_2H(a_2\xi-a_1)-c_3(a_2\xi-a_1)-L(a_{HX}\xi+a_{HZ})+H(a_{LX}\xi+a_{LZ})=0 \Leftrightarrow$$

$$L(c_1(a_2\xi-a_1)-(a_{HX}\xi+a_{HZ}))+H(c_2(a_2\xi-a_1)+(a_{LX}\xi+a_{LZ}))-c_3(a_2\xi-a_1)=0.$$

Defining $d_1=-(c_1(a_2\xi-a_1)-(a_{HX}\xi+a_{HZ}))$, $d_2=c_2(a_2\xi-a_1)+(a_{LX}\xi+a_{LZ})$ and $d_3=-c_3(a_2\xi-a_1)$ this equation can be written as $-d_1L+d_2H+d_3=0$ with positive constant coefficients d_i, $i=1,2,3$.

$d_1>0$ since $a_2\xi-a_1=a_{LR}a_{HX}\xi-a_{HR}a_{LX}\xi-a_{HR}a_{LZ}+a_{LR}a_{HZ}=$

$=a_{LR}(a_{HX}\xi+a_{HZ})-a_{HR}(a_{LX}\xi+a_{LZ})<0 \Leftrightarrow$

$\frac{a_{HX}\xi+a_{HZ}}{a_{LX}\xi+a_{LZ}}=\frac{H_X+H_Z}{L_X+L_Z}<h_R$ which is fulfilled under the assumed ranking of factor intensities.

$d_2>0$ since $d_2=c_2(a_2\xi-a_1)+(a_{LX}\xi+a_{LZ})=$

$=c_2(a_{LR}(a_{HX}\xi+a_{HZ})-a_{HR}(a_{LX}\xi+a_{LZ}))+(a_{LX}\xi+a_{LZ})=$

$$= c_2 a_{LR}\left(a_{HX}\xi + a_{HZ}\right) - \left(c_2 a_{HR} - 1\right)\left(a_{LX}\xi + a_{LZ}\right) =$$
$$= c_2 a_{LR}\left(a_{HX}\xi + a_{HZ}\right) + \left(1 - \eta(1-\theta)\delta\right)\left(a_{LX}\xi + a_{LZ}\right) > 0.$$

$d_3 > 0$ since $a_2\xi - a_1 < 0$.

Solving the iso-output ratio equation for H gives

$$H = -\frac{d_3}{d_2} + \frac{d_1}{d_2}L.$$

The graph of this function intersects the H-axis, for every endowment which ensures a positive growth rate, at a negative value of H.

7. Proof of proposition 2

To prove the proposition we will initially prove a lemma.

Lemma 1

If the factor intensities h^i for sectors $i = R, X, Z$ can be uniquely ranked such that $h_R > h_X > h_Z$ and all three sectors are active then $h_R > \frac{H}{L}$.

Proof

The factor intensities are defined as $h_i := \frac{H_i}{L_i}, i = R, X, Z$. By assumption $h_R > h_X > h_Z$. Thus $h_R L_R = H_R$, $h_R L_X > H_X$ and $h_R L_Z > H_Z$. Summing up these three equations yields $h_R\left(L_R + L_X + L_Z\right) > H_R + H_X + H_Z$ and we find

$$\frac{H}{L} = \frac{H_R + H_X + H_Z}{L_R + L_X + L_Z} < \frac{h_R\left(L_R + L_X + L_Z\right)}{L_R + L_X + L_Z} = h_R \qquad \Diamond$$

(a) The growth rate is given by (20). With constant prices and constant endowment we have $g'(\rho) = -\left(1 - \eta(1-\theta)\right) < 0$. $\Diamond$

(b) The output ratio is given by

$$\frac{X}{Z} = \frac{g(\rho)a_1 + a_{HZ}L - a_{LZ}H}{g(\rho)a_2 - a_{HX}L + a_{LX}H}$$

which after derivation yields

$$\frac{\partial(X/Z)}{\partial\rho} = \frac{g'(\rho)a_1\left(g(\rho)a_2 - a_{HX}L + a_{LX}H\right) - \left(g(\rho)a_1 + a_{HZ}L - a_{LZ}H\right)g'(\rho)a_2}{\left(g(\rho)\left(a_{LR}a_{HX} - a_{HR}a_{LX}\right) - a_{HX}L + a_{LX}H\right)^2} =$$

$$= \frac{g'(\rho)}{(\cdot)^2}\{H(a_1 a_{LX} + a_2 a_{LZ}) - L(a_1 a_{HX} + a_2 a_{HZ})L\}.$$

Reinserting a_1 and a_2 and rearranging gives

$$\frac{\partial(X/Z)}{\partial \rho} = \frac{g'(\rho)}{(\cdot)^2}(h_X - h_Z)a_{LX}a_{LZ}a_{LR}(H - Lh_R).$$

Since by assumption $h_X > h_Z$ and since we know that $g'(\rho) < 0$ we can conclude

$$\frac{\partial(X/Z)}{\partial \rho} > 0 \text{ if } h_R > \frac{H}{L},$$

which is fulfilled (cf. lemma) under the standard assumption of decreasing factor intensities. ◊

8. The split derivative

The first part

By dividing equation (A.13) through $L - a_{LR}g(\rho)$ we obtain

$$\frac{X}{Z} = \frac{a_{HZ} - \dfrac{H - a_{HR}g(\rho)}{L - a_{LR}g(\rho)}a_{LZ}}{a_{LX}\dfrac{H - a_{HR}g(\rho)}{L - a_{LR}g(\rho)} - a_{HX}}.$$

From this equation we find

$$\frac{\partial(X/Z)}{\partial\left(\dfrac{H - a_{HR}g(\rho)}{L - a_{LR}g(\rho)}\right)} = \frac{-a_{LZ}\left(a_{LX}\dfrac{H - a_{HR}g(\rho)}{L - a_{LR}g(\rho)} - a_{HX}\right) - a_{LX}\left(a_{HZ} - \dfrac{H - a_{HR}g(\rho)}{L - a_{LR}g(\rho)}a_{LZ}\right)}{\left(a_{LX}\dfrac{H - a_{HR}g(\rho)}{L - a_{LR}g(\rho)} - a_{HX}\right)^2} =$$

$$= a_{LZ}a_{LX}\frac{h_X - h_Z}{(\cdot)^2} > 0 \text{ if } h_X > h_Z.$$

The second part

$$\frac{\partial\left(\dfrac{H - a_{HR}g(\rho)}{L - a_{LR}g(\rho)}\right)}{\partial \rho} = \frac{a_{LR}g'(\rho)(H - a_{HR}g(\rho)) - a_{HR}g'(\rho)(L - a_{LR}g(\rho))}{(L - a_{LR}g(\rho))^2} > 0 \Leftrightarrow$$ [10]

$$\Leftrightarrow a_{LR}(H - a_{HR}g(\rho)) - a_{HR}(L - a_{LR}g(\rho)) < 0 \Leftrightarrow$$

10 note that $g'(\rho) < 0$

$$\Leftrightarrow \frac{a_{HR}}{a_{LR}} = h_R > \frac{H - a_{HR} g(\rho)}{L - a_{LR} g(\rho)}.$$

This condition is always fulfilled under the standard assumption of decreasing factor intensity (this proof is analogous to the proof of lemma 1).

9. Autarky wage ratio and factor endowment

Here we show that an increase of H (and a decrease of L) decreases the autarky factor reward ratio $\omega = w_H / w_L$.

The specification of a closed economy differs from the one of a small open economy only in the fact that now prices are determined by goods market clearing conditions. Thus we can start our analysis from (A.3). With explicit expressions for unit demands this becomes

$$a_{LR}(\cdot)g + \left((1-\gamma)\left(\frac{w_H}{w_L}\right)^{\gamma} \frac{\eta}{n^{(1-\theta)/\theta}} \frac{p_X}{p_D} + (1-\eta-\beta)\frac{p_X}{w_L} \right) X^S +$$

$$+ \left((1-\gamma)\left(\frac{w_H}{w_L}\right)^{\gamma} \frac{\eta}{n^{(1-\theta)/\theta}} \frac{p_Z}{p_D} + (1-\eta-\alpha)\frac{p_Z}{w_L} \right) Z^S = L,$$

$$a_{HR}(\cdot)g + \left(\gamma\left(\frac{w_L}{w_H}\right)^{1-\gamma} \frac{\eta}{n^{(1-\theta)/\theta}} \frac{p_X}{p_D} + \beta\frac{p_X}{w_H} \right) X^S +$$

$$+ \left(\gamma\left(\frac{w_L}{w_H}\right)^{1-\gamma} \frac{\eta}{n^{(1-\theta)/\theta}} \frac{p_Z}{p_D} + \alpha\frac{p_z}{w_H} \right) Z^S = H.$$

Inserting $p_D = n^{-\frac{1-\theta}{\theta}} \frac{w_H^{\gamma} w_L^{1-\gamma}}{\theta}$, $g = \frac{(1-\theta)\eta}{w_H^{\gamma} w_L^{1-\gamma}} - \rho$ (cf. (A.1) and (A.11)) - where we have chosen E as numeraire which implies constant wages but decreasing prices -, $a_{LR} = (1-\gamma)(w_H/w_L)^{\gamma}$ and $a_{HR} = \gamma(w_L/w_H)^{1-\gamma}$ gives

$$(1-\gamma)\left(\frac{w_H}{w_L}\right)^{\gamma}\left(\frac{(1-\theta)\eta}{w_H^{\gamma} w_L^{1-\gamma}} - \rho\right) + \left((1-\gamma)\eta\theta + 1 - \eta - \beta\right)\frac{p_X}{w_L} X^S +$$

$$+ \left((1-\gamma)\eta\theta + 1 - \eta - \alpha\right)\frac{p_Z}{w_L} Z^S = L,$$

$$\gamma\left(\frac{w_L}{w_H}\right)^{1-\gamma}\left(\frac{(1-\theta)\eta}{w_H^{\gamma} w_L^{1-\gamma}} - \rho\right) + (\gamma\eta\theta + \beta)\frac{p_X}{w_H} X^S + (\gamma\eta\theta + \alpha)\frac{p_Z}{w_H} Z^S = H.$$

Now assume Cobb-Douglas utility functions which imply an allocation of a fraction σ of total expenditure (normalized to unity) to good X and the remaining fraction $1\text{-}\sigma$ to good Z. Rearranging yields

$$f_1(w_L, w_H) := c_1/w_L - (1-\gamma)(w_H/w_L)^\gamma \rho - L = 0,$$
$$f_2(w_L, w_H) := c_2/w_H - \gamma(w_L/w_H)^{1-\gamma} \rho - H = 0,$$

with

$$c_1 = (1-\gamma)(1-\theta)\eta + ((1-\gamma)\eta\theta + 1 - \eta - \beta)\sigma + ((1-\gamma)\eta\theta + 1 - \eta - \alpha)(1-\sigma),$$
$$c_2 = \gamma(1-\theta)\eta + (\gamma\eta\theta + \beta)\sigma + (\gamma\eta\theta + \alpha)(1-\sigma).$$

These two equations are the starting point of our proof. As cannot be easily seen, the subsequent analysis simplifies considerably if we multiply both equations by $(-w_L)$ and $(-w_H)$, respectively. This yields with $(\cdot)$ replacing (w_L, w_H)

$$\begin{aligned} g_1(\cdot) &:= -c_1 + (1-\gamma) w_H^\gamma w_L^{1-\gamma} \rho + w_L L = -c_1 + (1-\gamma)\rho c_R(\cdot) + w_L L = 0, \\ g_2(\cdot) &:= -c_2 + \gamma w_L^{1-\gamma} w_H^\gamma \rho + w_H H = -c_2 + \gamma \rho c_R(\cdot) + w_H H = 0. \end{aligned} \tag{A.14}$$

Now with the help of the implicit function theorem we can derive the change of factor rewards with respect to a change of the human capital stock (cf. e.g. Chiang, 1974, pp. 222 - 225). This then gives $\partial w_L/\partial H = |J_L|/|J|$ and $\partial w_H/\partial H = |J_H|/|J|$ with

$$|J| = \begin{vmatrix} \partial g_1(\cdot)/\partial w_L & \partial g_1(\cdot)/\partial w_H \\ \partial g_2(\cdot)/\partial w_L & \partial g_2(\cdot)/\partial w_H \end{vmatrix}, \qquad |J_L| = \begin{vmatrix} -\partial g_1(\cdot)/\partial H & \partial g_1(\cdot)/\partial w_H \\ -\partial g_2(\cdot)/\partial H & \partial g_2(\cdot)/\partial w_H \end{vmatrix},$$

$$|J_H| = \begin{vmatrix} \partial g_1(\cdot)/\partial w_L & -\partial g_1(\cdot)/\partial H \\ \partial g_2(\cdot)/\partial w_L & -\partial g_2(\cdot)/\partial H \end{vmatrix}.$$

The partial derivatives are given by

$$\partial g_1(\cdot)/\partial w_L = (1-\gamma)\rho a_{LR}(\cdot) + L, \qquad \partial g_1(\cdot)/\partial w_H = (1-\gamma)\rho a_{HR}(\cdot),$$
$$\partial g_2(\cdot)/\partial w_L = \gamma \rho a_{LR}(\cdot), \qquad \partial g_2(\cdot)/\partial w_H = \gamma \rho a_{HR}(\cdot) + hL,$$
$$\partial g_1(\cdot)/\partial H = 0, \qquad \partial g_2(\cdot)/\partial h = w_H.$$

The value of the determinants is

$$|J| = ((1-\gamma)\rho a_{LR}(\cdot) + L)(\gamma\rho a_{HR}(\cdot) + H) - \gamma\rho a_{LR}(\cdot)(1-\gamma)\rho a_{HR}(\cdot) =$$
$$= (1-\gamma)\rho a_{LR}(\cdot)\gamma\rho a_{HR}(\cdot) + L\gamma\rho a_{HR}(\cdot) + (1-\gamma)\rho a_{LR}(\cdot)H + LH - \gamma(1-\gamma)\rho^2 a_{LR}(\cdot)a_{HR}(\cdot) =$$
$$= L\gamma\rho a_{HR}(\cdot) + (1-\gamma)\rho a_{LR}(\cdot)H + LH > 0.$$
$$|J_L| = w_H(1-\gamma)\rho a_{HR}(\cdot) > 0.$$
$$|J_H| = -((1-\gamma)\rho a_{LR}(\cdot) + L)Lw_H < 0.$$

Now we can compute

$$\frac{\partial(w_H/w_L)}{\partial H}=\frac{\frac{\partial w_H}{\partial H}w_L-\frac{\partial w_L}{\partial H}w_H}{w_L^2}<0\Leftrightarrow\frac{\partial w_H/\partial H}{\partial w_L/\partial H}<\frac{w_H}{w_L}\Leftrightarrow\frac{|J_H|}{|J_L|}<\frac{w_H}{w_L}.$$

which is always fulfilled since the LHS of the last inequality is negative. Thus $\frac{\partial(w_H/w_L)}{\partial H}<0$. ◊

By analogy we can prove $-\frac{\partial(w_H/w_L)}{\partial L}<0$.

10. Proof of proposition 3

We start our investigation with (A. 14). The change of factor rewards with respect to a change of the individual discount rate is given by $\partial w_L/\partial\rho=|J_L|/|J|$ and $\partial w_H/\partial\rho=|J_H|/|J|$ with $|J|=L\gamma\rho a_{HR}(\cdot)+(1-\gamma)\rho a_{LR}(\cdot)H+LH>0$ as before and

$$|J_L|=\begin{vmatrix}-\partial g_1(\cdot)/\partial\rho & \partial g_1(\cdot)/\partial w_H\\ -\partial g_2(\cdot)/\partial\rho & \partial g_2(\cdot)/\partial w_H\end{vmatrix},\qquad |J_H|=\begin{vmatrix}\partial g_1(\cdot)/\partial w_L & -\partial g_1(\cdot)/\partial\rho\\ \partial g_2(\cdot)/\partial w_L & -\partial g_2(\cdot)/\partial\rho\end{vmatrix}.$$

The partial derivatives are given by

$$\partial g_1(\cdot)/\partial w_L=(1-\gamma)\rho a_{LR}(\cdot)+L,\qquad \partial g_1(\cdot)/\partial w_H=(1-\gamma)\rho a_{HR}(\cdot),$$
$$\partial g_2(\cdot)/\partial w_L=\gamma\rho a_{LR}(\cdot),\qquad \partial g_2(\cdot)/\partial w_H=\gamma\rho a_{HR}(\cdot)+H,$$
$$\partial g_1(\cdot)/\partial\rho=(1-\gamma)c_R(\cdot),\qquad \partial g_2(\cdot)/\partial\rho=\gamma c_R(\cdot).$$

which allows to compute the determinants as

$$\begin{aligned}|J_L|&=-(1-\gamma)c_R(\cdot)(\gamma\rho a_{HR}(\cdot)+H)+\gamma c_R(\cdot)(1-\gamma)\rho a_{HR}(\cdot)\\&=-\gamma(1-\gamma)\rho c_R(\cdot)a_{HR}(\cdot)-(1-\gamma)c_R(\cdot)H+\gamma(1-\gamma)\rho c_R(\cdot)a_{HR}(\cdot)\\&=-(1-\gamma)c_R(\cdot)H<0,\\|J_H|&=-((1-\gamma)\rho a_{LR}(\cdot)+L)\gamma c_R(\cdot)+\gamma\rho a_{LR}(\cdot)(1-\gamma)c_R(\cdot)\\&=-\gamma(1-\gamma)\rho a_{LR}(\cdot)c_R(\cdot)-L\gamma c_R(\cdot)+\gamma(1-\gamma)\rho a_{LR}(\cdot)c_R(\cdot)\\&=-L\gamma c_R(\cdot)<0.\end{aligned}$$

Thus both factor rewards are decreasing in ρ.

Now we need the change of the ratio of factor rewards with respect to a change of ρ. It is given by

$$\frac{\partial(w_H/w_L)}{\partial\rho}=\frac{\frac{\partial w_H}{\partial\rho}w_L-\frac{\partial w_L}{\partial\rho}w_H}{w_L^2}<0 \text{ if (note that } \partial w_L/\partial\rho<0)$$

$$\frac{\partial w_H/\partial\rho}{\partial w_L/\partial\rho}>\frac{w_H}{w_L}\Leftrightarrow\frac{|J_H|}{|J_L|}=\frac{L}{H}\frac{\gamma}{1-\gamma}>\frac{w_H}{w_L}\Leftrightarrow\frac{H}{L}<\frac{\gamma}{1-\gamma}\frac{w_L}{w_H}. \qquad \text{(A.15)}$$

From dividing the first order conditions of the cost minimization problem

$$\min_{H_R,L_R} w_L L_R + w_H H_R \quad s.t. \quad g_0 H_R^{\gamma} L_R^{1-\gamma}=g,$$

we obtain the well-known condition for an optimal employment of resources

$$\frac{w_H}{w_L}=\frac{\gamma}{1-\gamma}\frac{L_R}{H_R},$$

which is equivalent to $\frac{\gamma}{1-\gamma}\frac{w_L}{w_H}=h_R$. Inserted into (A.15) yields

$$\frac{\partial(w_H/w_L)}{\partial\rho}>0\Leftrightarrow\frac{H}{L}<h_R.$$

Finally with lemma 1 we have

$$\frac{\partial(w_H/w_L)}{\partial\rho}<0 \text{ if } h_R>h_x>h_Z. \qquad \Diamond$$

Chapter 6: Trade pattern reversal: The role of technological change, factor accumulation and government intervention

1. Introduction

Since the end of World War II some East Asian countries have undergone a rapid economic change. The Four Tigers and Japan are leading in average per-capita GDP growth in the period of 1960-1985, which, to a large extent, is attributable to a physical and human capital accumulation process, taking place at a significantly faster pace than in other countries[1]. As a consequence, some countries which formerly were exporters of labour intensive goods have witnessed a change of their trade relations and are now high-tech exporters. Empirical evidence is reported e.g. for Japan by Grossman (1990) and Balassa and Noland (1989). Few theoretical investigations are undertaken of how to explain the mechanisms of such a reversal of trade relations, except Grossman and Helpman (1991a, ch. 7) and Grossman (1990). In these models, however, a change of trade patterns is explained by an *exogenous* change in the endowment of human capital which does not allow to study the mechanisms, how such a change in endowment takes place, and, most importantly, why it takes place at a faster pace than in other countries. It is the aim of this chapter to study more in detail under which circumstances trade patterns reverse.

There are certainly many factors which influence the evolution of the production structure and thereby the trade pattern of a country. Having the experience of Japan or the Four Tigers in mind, we focus on two of the most important ones (cf. e.g. Lucas, 1993, who discusses many aspects related to the economic success of the Four Tigers): Endogenous technological change and human capital accumulation. As a consequence, trade patterns will be determined by the interaction of Ricardian as well as Heckscher-Ohlin effects. The next section presents a two-country world with endogenous technological change and human capital accumulation, thus combining two "engines of growth": Human capital accumulation as in Lucas (1988) and a public knowledge stock as in Grossman and

---

[1] For a comprehensive study of the "East Asian miracle", cf. World Bank (1993).

Helpman (1991a). The third section studies the stability properties of the model, drawing a distinction between three cases: a world in which either Ricardian or Heckscher-Ohlin features dominate and a world where both effects interact. The subsequent section then gives sufficient conditions for a reversal of trade patterns. In the fifth section, the influence of government intervention on the evolution of the economies is studied. We allow both for subsidies for the R&D activity and measures which increase the human capital accumulation capacity. Again, conditions for a reversal of trade patterns are derived for the different cases. Finally, the sixth section completes the findings on trade pattern reversal and discusses under which conditions an initially poor country (measured in terms of per capita consumption) can increase its share in world consumption.

2. A two-country world

The theoretical growth literature has put forward many different explanations for long-run positive growth rates. One distinguishes between models based on technological progress (Solow, 1956), learning-by-doing (Romer, 1986), human capital accumulation (Lucas, 1988), public stocks of knowledge (Romer, 1990; Grossman and Helpman, 1990), public infrastructure (Barro, 1990) or linearities in the production function (Romer, 1987; Rebelo, 1991). Trying to capture essential features of a catching-up process of East Asian countries, however, requires to allow for several endogenous changes, both of technology and of stocks of production factors. Differences in technology could be modelled easiest by assuming different productivity factors, which, however, would not allow to discuss an endogenous change of technology. Thus we model the state of the technology by the depth of the division of labour, and use the specification proposed by Ethier (1982), which is the analogue to the Dixit and Stiglitz (1977) formulation in consumption theory. With this specification, technological progress is equivalent to an increase of the number of intermediate goods.

The world economy we consider consists of two countries and trades in final goods, but does not allow for international financial capital movements and trade in intermediate goods. For convenience, we assume that both countries remain incompletely specialized after opening up to trade.

Consumption side

For modelling the consumption side, we choose the Lucas (1988) framework extended to two consumption goods. We first characterize the behaviour of a household *i*, living in country *j*, and then aggregate over all households of that country.

Since the scope of the model is not to study the effects of disconnectedness between individuals or cohorts (Blanchard, 1985; Weil, 1987; Buiter, 1988) we assume a bequest motive à la Barro (1974) and thus let members of household *i* maximize at time *t* the discounted stream of future utility with an infinite horizon which can be expressed by

$$U^i(t)=\int_t^\infty \exp[-\rho(\tau-t)]u^i(\tau)d\tau, \tag{1}$$

where the time preference rate is given by ρ. Instantaneous felicity u^i results from the consumption of two final homogenous goods X^i and Z^i. It is expressed in the log form as $u^i(\tau)=\log\left[X^{i\sigma}Z^{i1-\sigma}\right]$, where $0<\sigma<1$. Note that preferences are assumed to be identical across countries, both with respect to intertemporal issues (the time preference rate) and with respect to demand for final goods. Static utility maximization implies standard demand functions for final goods, depending on consumer *i*'s total expenditure $E^i(t)$ and on prices p_X and p_Z,

$$X^i=\frac{\sigma}{p_X}E^i(t), \qquad Z^i=\frac{1-\sigma}{p_Z}E^i(t). \tag{2}$$

Now reinsert these static optimality conditions into (1) and maximize the modified utility function with respect to the share of human capital allocated to production $\mu^i(t)$ and total expenditure $E^i(t)$, subject to a flow budget constraint and a human capital accumulation constraint which read

$$E^i(t)+\dot{A}^i(t)=r^j(t)A^i(t)+\phi\iota^i(t)+w_L^j(t)+w_H^j(t)\mu^i(t)H^i(t), \tag{3}$$

$$\dot{H}^i(t)=H^i(t)\delta(1-\mu^i(t)). \tag{4}$$

The first constraint equates expenditures and the change of the value of assets, household *i* holds, $\dot{A}^i(t)$, to asset, R&D, labour and human capital income, $r^j(t)A^i(t)$, $\phi\iota^i$, $w_L^j(t)$ and $w_H^j(t)\mu^i(t)H^i(t)$, where each household owns one unit of labour and allocates a share $\mu^i(t) \in]0,1]$ of human capital to production[2, 3]. The second constraint relates the remaining human capital share $1-\mu^i(t)$ to the human capital accumulation process. Equation (4) can be read in two ways: Either one argues that it represents a production function which says that the stock of human capital increases if some human capital is allocated in an education sector, or the factor $\mu^i(t)$ indicates how people spend their *time* between working and autodidactic activities, such as reading.

The outcome of the above individual maximization procedure can be easily aggregated over all households of one country. Since preferences (ρ) and human capital accumulation capabilities (the "productivity of reading" δ) are by assumption identical for all households in both countries and the interest rate $r^j(t)$ and factor rewards $w_H^j(t)$ are exogenously given, every household of country j behaves the same. Thus we find as optimality conditions for the behaviour of the economy as a whole (with the time index suppressed and the country index j replacing the household index i) (cf. appendix)

$$\frac{\dot{E}^j}{E^j} = r^j - \rho, \tag{5}$$

$$\frac{\dot{w}_H^j}{w_H^j} = r^j - \delta, \tag{6}$$

and as aggregate accumulation constraints

$$E^j + \dot{A}^j = r^j A^j + \phi \iota^j + w_L^j L^j + w_H^j \mu^j H^j, \tag{7}$$

$$\dot{H}^j = H^j \delta(1-\mu^j). \tag{8}$$

Some remarks can already be made with respect to the outcome of the model, given these equations. Provided that interest rates equalize internationally, by (5) each country will experience the same growth of aggregate expenditure, a result emphasized by Rebelo (1992). This means that, given internationally perfectly mobile financial capital, the rate of growth of consumption per capita is completely independent of the production side (in contrast to, of course, the *level* of consumption per capita). Internationally completely mobile capital, however, is not

2 The source of R&D income amounting to $\phi \iota^i$ on the individual and $\phi \iota^j$ on the economy level will become clear when discussing the R&D process.

3 Being based on Grossman-Helpman models, we do not have a transformation process between (unskilled) labour and human capital. The stock of labour is exogenously given and does not change when the economic environment of the agents changes. How this could be modelled is shown in Grossman and Helpman (1991a, ch. 5.2).

a necessary condition for "consumption growth rate equalization": Assume that the endowment of both countries is such that neither country specializes; then factor prices equalize and, by equation (6), interest rates equalize – even with internationally immobile capital – which, again, implies identical growth rates of consumption per capita.

In addition to the dynamic optimality conditions and constraints, aggregate world demand functions for final goods have to be added. They are given by

$$X^D = \frac{\sigma}{p_X}\left(E^A + E^B\right), \qquad Z^D = \frac{1-\sigma}{p_Z}\left(E^A + E^B\right).$$

Production side

Two final homogenous goods X and Z are produced, using human capital and labour, given a certain technology level. Since technology changes over time, the specification of how technology influences the productivity of human capital and labour, is crucial for the outcome of the model. Two extreme examples help to illustrate the possibilities: Either technological progress increases the productivity of human capital and labour to the same extent (cf. chapter 5 or Grossman and Helpman, 1991a, ch. 6) or only one factor enjoys higher productivity, leaving the other factor unaffected. In a two-country world, the first specification would not be very interesting: The technological level of a country would simply determine the country's income level, but would not exert any influence on trade patterns. Consequently, Ricardian effects would be missing in the model and a simultaneous study of technological change and factor accumulation would not give further insights. Therefore, we take here the second approach and assume that the technological level increases the productivity of (unskilled) labour only[4]. The basic structure of the production side of the economy is thus given by three activities: Production of two final homogenous goods and of differentiated middle goods.

---

[4] There is a further - technical - necessity why technological progress has to be restricted to labour only: The rate of innovation in models à la Grossman and Helpman is an increasing function of a country's factor endowment. Thus, if the stock of human capital influenced technological progress, we would obtain ever increasing rates of growth which is hard to justify on an empirical basis.

The production of the consumption goods follows Cobb-Douglas production functions with constant returns to scale in two inputs, human capital H and a set of intermediate goods k, represented by an index K,

$$Z^j = Z_0\left(H_Z^j\right)^{\alpha}\left(K_Z^j\right)^{1-\alpha}, \tag{9}$$

$$X^j = X_0\left(H_X^j\right)^{\beta}\left(K_X^j\right)^{1-\beta}. \tag{10}$$

Without loss of generality, we assume that the output elasticity of X with respect to H is higher than the output elasticity of Z with respect to H: $\beta > \alpha$. Perfect competition ensures zero-profits which can be expressed by equality of prices and unit costs. Further, since consumption goods are perfect substitutes, independently of their country of origin, free trade equalizes goods prices and unit costs must satisfy, as long as both countries are incompletely specialized

$$p_Z = \left(w_H^j\right)^{\alpha}\left(w_K^j\right)^{1-\alpha},$$

$$p_X = \left(w_H^j\right)^{\beta}\left(w_K^j\right)^{1-\beta}.$$

The price index w_K reflects the prices of intermediates necessary to obtain one unit of K. The constants X_0 and Z_0 have been suitably chosen to obtain these unit cost functions. As is well-known, these pricing conditions imply factor price equalization in w_H and w_K, since linear homogenous Cobb-Douglas production functions exclude factor intensity reversals.

The production process in the consumption good sectors specified in (9) and (10) has to be understood that firms employ human capital in order to assemble varieties k to obtain final output X or Z. The index K is given by, similar to Ethier (1982),

$$K^j = \left(\int_0^{n^j}\left(y^k\right)^{\theta}dk\right)^{1/\theta}, \qquad 0<\theta<1. \tag{11}$$

This index increases in the (measure of the) number n^j of intermediate goods k available in country j, which allows to represent technological progress in the production of X and Z by an increase in the range of intermediate goods. The higher n^j, the larger the range of inputs and the higher the output of consumption goods.

Intermediate goods k are produced in a setting of monopolistic competition. Firms producing either X or Z then choose among intermediate goods optimally by minimizing total costs $\int_0^{n^j} p_y^k y^k dk$ with respect to y^k subject to (11). This gives demand for each variety of the form (cf. appendix, chapter 5)

$$y^k = \left(p_y^k\right)^{-1/(1-\theta)} K^j \left(\int_0^{n^j} \left(p_y^k\right)^{-\theta/(1-\theta)} dk\right)^{-1/\theta}. \tag{12}$$

The production of varieties of the middle goods consists of two steps. Due to, e.g., infinite patent protection, each producer of intermediate goods, as the first step, has to develop her own blueprint for producing a new variety. This R&D process is described by a simple cost function which reads for a firm producing variety k

$$c_R^k = \phi / (Kn)^k .$$

This equation basically says that the development of a new blueprint requires the spending of some fixed costs ϕ (a similar specification was used by Barro and Sala-i-Martin, 1992) divided by the total non-appropriable stock of public knowledge accessible for firm k. Clearly, this is the Romer (1990) idea of technological spillovers which results from the R&D process as a by-product to the development of new blueprints, an idea used extensively by Grossman and Helpman (1991a).

It is well-known, that those spillovers resulting from R&D can result in positive long-run innovation rates. Since in the present model, technological change relies on that mechanism, a further, very important assumption about *inter*national spillovers has to be made in a context of a two-country world. Information which flows freely between countries leads to innovation rate equalization (Rivera-Batiz and Romer, 1991; Grossman and Helpman, 1991a, ch.7; 1991b, section 6). On the other hand, if knowledge diffusion is restricted to the national market, then the world economy is characterized by hysteresis effects (Grossman and Helpman, 1991a, ch.8; Feenstra, 1990; Devereux and Lapham, 1993). It seems unrealistic to assume that the rate of technological progress equalizes automatically across countries; thus we prefer the second specification where the public knowledge stock is restricted to the country where it was build up. This implies innovation rates which differ normally between countries[5].

Relating the public knowledge stock to the number of differentiated goods available in country j, restricted R&D spillovers translate into an expression for

[5] Different innovation rates due to restricted knowledge flows are also obtained by Rivera-Batiz and Xie (1993). Other possibilities to model growth rates which differ between countries are, e.g., Buiter and Kletzer (1991), Alogoskoufis and van der Ploeg (1991a,b).

R&D costs of ϕ/n^j instead of $\phi/(n^A + n^B)$, which would be the case if we had international knowledge spillovers. Consequently, the intertemporal zero-profit condition reads

$$\phi/n^j = v^j(t) = \int_t^{\infty} \exp\left[-\left(R^j(\tau) - R^j(t)\right)\right]\pi^j(\tau)d\tau, \tag{13}$$

where current profits $\pi^j(\tau)$ are discounted by a cumulative factor $R^j(u) = \int_0^u r^j(s)ds$ depending on the interest rate $r^j(s)$. Note, that R&D costs as in (13) which firms have to pay, flow back to consumers and thus generate income, amounting, at the economy level, to $\dot{n}^j\,\phi/n^j = \phi\,\iota^j$, as included in the economy's budget constraint (7).

The production of the intermediate goods follows a simple constant-returns-to-scale production function $y^k = L^k$ and producers, facing demand function (12), set profit maximizing prices above marginal costs (cf. appendix, chapter 2)

$$p_y^j = \frac{w_L^j}{\theta}, \tag{14}$$

which implies current profits amounting to $\pi^j = (1-\theta)p_y^j y^j = (1-\theta)\dfrac{w_L^j}{\theta}\dfrac{L^{D^j}}{n^j}$.

Since all firms of country j have to pay the same labour rewards w_L^j, equation (14) implies that all varieties produced in that country are equally priced at p_y^j. The expression for costs of the set of intermediate goods necessary to obtain one unit of K therefore takes a simple form. Inserting (12) into the cost function $\int_0^{n^j} p_y^k y^k dk$ and using (14) gives costs as a function of labour rewards and the technological level of the economy (cf. appendix chapter 5),

$$w_K^j = \left(\int_0^{n^j} \left(p_y^j\right)^{\theta/(\theta-1)} dk\right)^{-(1-\theta)/\theta} = \left(n^j\right)^{-(1-\theta)/\theta}\frac{w_L^j}{\theta}.$$

Market equilibria

By equation (12), equal prices for all intermediate goods lead to equal output per variety. Thus, aggregate demand for labour can be simply expressed as a function of demand for intermediate inputs as

$$L^{D^j} = n^j y^j = Y^j. \tag{15}$$

Demand for intermediate goods, in turn, depends on the total quantity of K used in the production process of consumption goods, since by (11)

$$K^j = \left(n^j\right)^{1/\theta} y^j = \left(n^j\right)^{(1-\theta)/\theta} Y^j.$$

Finally, since the index K is related to final output of consumption goods X and Z by

$$a_{KX}\left(w_H^j, w_K^j\right)X^j + a_{KZ}\left(w_H^j, w_K^j\right)Z^j = K^j, \tag{16}$$

where $a_{K\cdot}(w_H, w_K)$ are unit factor demand functions, the full employment condition for labour reads

$$a_{KX}\left(w_H^j, w_K^j\right)X^j + a_{KZ}\left(w_H^j, w_K^j\right)Z^j = L^j\left(n^j\right)^{(1-\theta)/\theta}. \tag{17}$$

The supply of human capital for production is subject to the households' trade-off between production and accumulation of human capital; the quantity $\mu^j H^j$ used for production is then further subdivided between production of final goods,

$$a_{HX}\left(w_H^j, w_K^j\right)X^j + a_{HZ}\left(w_H^j, w_K^j\right)Z^j = \mu^j H^j. \tag{18}$$

3. Solution of the model and dynamic properties

Reduced form

In order to derive the reduced form of the model presented above, one first solves for human capital rewards and the price index for intermediate goods with the help of clearing conditions for factor markets and goods markets and pricing conditions for final goods[6]. This gives (a full derivation of all steps necessary to obtain the reduced form can be found in the appendix)

$$w_K = \frac{c_L}{\left(n^A\right)^{\frac{1-\theta}{\theta}} L^A + \left(n^B\right)^{\frac{1-\theta}{\theta}} L^B} E, \qquad w_H = \frac{1-c_L}{\mu^A H^A + \mu^B H^B} E,$$

where $c_L \in]0,1[$ is a constant, representing preference and technology parameters. Then the budget constraints are simplified by inserting factor rewards, w_K and w_H, and the financial capital market no-arbitrage condition which can be obtained by differentiating (13) with respect to time. It turns out that one budget constraint is always fulfilled if the other one is satisfied (which is the verification of Walras' law). This allows us to choose total expenditure as numeraire which implies, since by (6) interest rates equalize given incomplete specialization, $r = \rho$. Finally, the remaining budget constraint and the expression giving the factor reward for human

6 Note that factor rewards can be computed explicitly only in the case of factor prices equalization in w_H and w_K. This is given as long as both countries are incompletely specialized.

capital is differentiated with respect to time and the resulting equations can be solved to yield

$$\dot{\mu}^A = f(\Omega)\left(\mu^A + \mu^B \Lambda\right) + \mu^A\left(\mu^A \delta - \rho\right), \tag{19}$$

$$\dot{\mu}^B = -f(\Omega)\left(\mu^A \Lambda^{-1} + \mu^B\right) + \mu^B\left(\mu^B \delta - \rho\right), \tag{20}$$

where, for notational convenience, we defined the ratios of the number of varieties and of the stock of human capital between countries as $\Omega := n^B / n^A$ and $\Lambda := H^B / H^A$, respectively, and

$$f(\Omega) := \frac{c_L^2}{(1-c_L)} \frac{(1-\theta)^2}{\phi\theta} L^A L^B \Omega^{\frac{1-\theta}{\theta}} \left(\Omega^{\frac{1-\theta}{\theta}} L^B - L^A\right)\left(L^A + \Omega^{\frac{1-\theta}{\theta}} L^B\right)^{-3}.$$

Due to the simple R&D structure, we can derive an explicit expressions for the rate of innovation of country *j* which turns out to be

$$\iota^j = (1-\theta) \frac{\left(n^j\right)^{\frac{1-\theta}{\theta}} L^j}{\left(n^A\right)^{\frac{1-\theta}{\theta}} L^A + \left(n^B\right)^{\frac{1-\theta}{\theta}} L^B} \frac{c_L}{\phi} - \rho. \tag{21}$$

It is an increasing function of each country's productivity-adjusted labour endowment $\left(n^j\right)^{\frac{1-\theta}{\theta}} L^j$ and decreases in the fixed component of R&D costs ϕ, in consumers' time preference rate ρ and in θ. A value of θ close to unity indicates a high elasticity of substitution (given by $\varepsilon = 1/(1-\theta)$; cf. equation (11)) between any two varieties. Thus the higher θ, the less an additional variety contributes to an increase of output and the lower the innovation rate.

Analyzing further, one finds that the outcome of the model does not depend on absolute quantities of differentiated goods or human capital, but on their ratios Ω and Λ only. The reduced form of the model is therefore completed by giving the evolution of Ω and Λ over time which turns out to read, by using the human capital accumulation constraint (8) and the innovation rate of country *j*,

$$\dot{\Lambda} = \delta\left(\mu^A - \mu^B\right)\Lambda, \tag{22}$$

$$\dot{\Omega} = (1-\theta) \frac{c_L}{\phi} \frac{\Omega^{\frac{1-\theta}{\theta}} L^B - L^A}{L^A + \Omega^{\frac{1-\theta}{\theta}} L^B} \Omega. \tag{23}$$

Thus the relatively simple reduced form consists of four equations only: (19), (20), (22) and (23).

Stability analysis

In analyzing the stability of the model, we first focus our attention on human capital accumulation alone and thus exclude (relative) technological change. Then, only technological change is taken into consideration before, finally, the interaction of technological change and human capital accumulation is studied.

No relative technological change – In the present framework, no relative technological change occurs (and thus Ricardian effects vanish) if the ratio of differentiated goods equals a fixed number given by the countries' labour endowment: $\dot{\Omega}=0 \Leftrightarrow n^B/n^A=\left(L^A/L^B\right)^{-\frac{1-\theta}{\theta}}$. In the subsequent analysis we will assume that this holds. Note, however, that the results which will turn out are not restricted to this, admittedly, rather special case, but are valid equally if e.g. technological spillovers would be excluded or the model would be specified with identical technologies right from the outset.

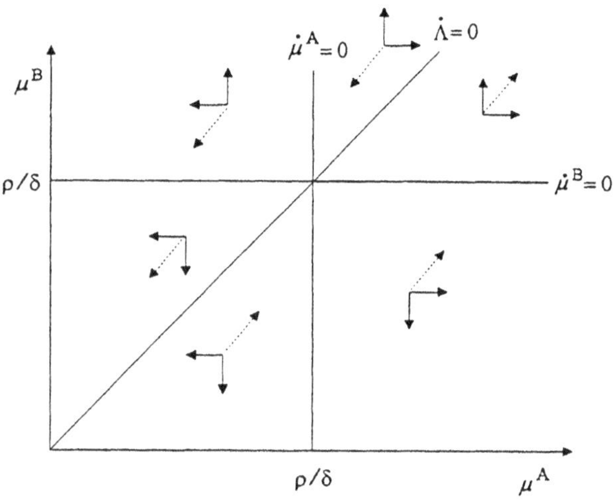

Figure 6.1: The decision problem with no technological change

If $\dot{\Omega}=0$, $f(\Omega)=0$ and equation (23) can be neglected. The economy is on a balanced growth path, defined by (19), (20) and (22), for $\mu^i=\rho/\delta$. The stability properties of such an equilibrium are easily analyzed by graphical phase plane analysis in the $\left(\mu^A,\mu^B\right)$ space, where solid arrows indicate the direction of motion of μ^i and dotted arrows pointing up- or downwards indicate an in- or decrease of Λ (imagine a third dimension): Note that both shares of human capital allocated to production, μ^A and μ^B, are control variables. If one of the countries decided to choose as initial value, right after opening up to trade, a point which does *not* satisfy $\mu^i = \rho/\delta$, then either μ^A or μ^B must eventually hit one of the boundaries $\{0,1\}$. Then the optimality condition (6) could no longer be satisfied. Consequently, provided both countries want to maximize current utility, they both choose at once the equilibrium values $\mu^A = \mu^B = \rho/\delta$[7].

No human capital accumulation – This would simplify the model to such an extent that one would no longer have to worry about stability properties. The optimal share of allocation of human capital between education and production would no longer be an issue and the model would be a simplified version of the hysteresis model of Grossman and Helpman (1991a, ch.8).

Technological change and human capital accumulation – Let us now turn to the certainly most interesting case where technological change and human capital accumulation interact. Assume that initial conditions are such that $\dot{\Omega} \geq 0 \; \forall t$ which implies $f(\Omega) > 0$[8]. Then the innovation rate of country B approaches its autarky innovation rate

$$\iota^B = (1-\theta)\frac{L^B}{\Omega^{-\frac{1-\theta}{\theta}}L^A + L^B}\frac{c_L}{\phi} - \rho \xrightarrow[\Omega\to\infty]{} (1-\theta)\frac{c_L}{\phi} - \rho, \tag{24}$$

and the innovation rate of country A becomes zero (in finite time!) since

$$\iota^A = (1-\theta)\frac{L^A}{L^A + \Omega^{\frac{1-\theta}{\theta}}L^B}\frac{c_L}{\phi} - \rho \geq 0 \Leftrightarrow \Omega^{\frac{1-\theta}{\theta}} \leq \left(\frac{1-\theta}{\phi}\frac{c_L}{\rho} - 1\right)\frac{L^A}{L^B}. \tag{25}$$

The innovation rate of country j was shown in (21) to be a function of its relative size (measured in effective labour endowment) in the world economy. If innovation in country B is higher than in the other country, its effective labour endowment $(n^B)^{\frac{1-\theta}{\theta}} L^B$ increases absolutely and relatively to the other country and, as a

7 It will be shown later that equilibrium values fall within the required interval $]0,1[$.

8 Making the opposite assumption $\dot{\Omega} \leq 0 \; \forall t$ would lead to a completely symmetrical analysis where country A has been renamed country B and vice versa.

corollary, the relative effective size of the other country decreases. Then, however, at a certain point in time, country A's effective labour endowment is too small to sustain positive innovation rates[9].

Since Ω is a monotonous function in time, we can divide equations (19) - (22) by equation (23) and thereby obtain a non-autonomous three dimensional system in Ω, which can be treated by graphical means. To this end, determine the zero-motion loci by setting the equations of motion equal to zero. This gives (cf. appendix)

$$\dot{\mu}^A \geq 0 \Leftrightarrow \mu^B \geq -\frac{\mu^A}{\Lambda}\left(\left(\mu^A\delta-\rho\right)f(\Omega)^{-1}+1\right), \tag{26}$$

$$\dot{\mu}^B \geq 0 \Leftrightarrow \mu^A \leq \mu^B\Lambda\left(\left(\mu^B\delta-\rho\right)f(\Omega)^{-1}-1\right), \tag{27}$$

$$\dot{\Lambda} \geq 0 \Leftrightarrow \mu^A \geq \mu^B. \tag{28}$$

Obviously, the function $f(\Omega)$ plays a crucial role for the dynamic properties of the model. Its extrema $\hat{\Omega}$ are given by (cf. appendix)

$$\hat{\Omega}_{1,2} = \left(\frac{L^A}{L^B}\left(2\pm\sqrt{3}\right)\right)^{\frac{\theta}{1-\theta}}.$$

The function $f(\Omega)$ approaches zero as Ω goes to infinity: $f(\Omega)\xrightarrow[\Omega\to\infty]{}0$ and its value at the origin is zero: $f(0)=0$. Since it is positive iff $\Omega>\left(L^A/L^B\right)^{\frac{\theta}{1-\theta}}$, a typical representation of $f(\Omega)$ can be plotted as in figure 6.2.

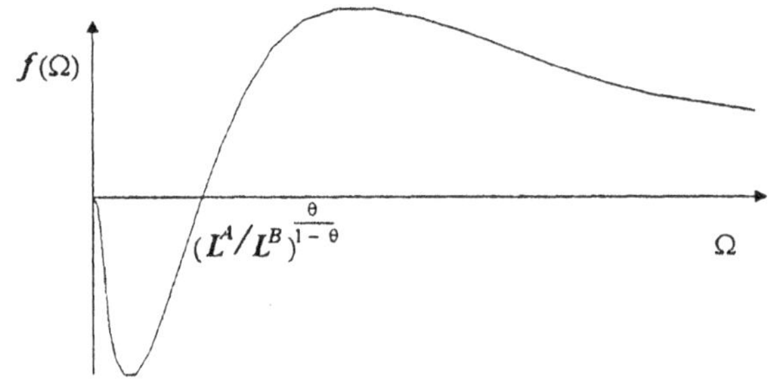

Figure 6.2: The technology function $f(\Omega)$

[9] This is the crucial difference to models with *international* spillovers of knowledge. In this case the innovation rates of both countries would equalise and depend on the *sum* of the effective labour endowment of both countries.

After this analysis of the technology function, we can plot the zero-motion loci for a certain $\Omega = \overline{\Omega}$ in figure 6.3, taking into consideration only the loci falling broadly within the range of $\mu^j \in]0,1]$[10]. The planes are determined by equations (26), (28) and the upper branch of (27), solved for μ^B, which is given by

$$\mu^B = \frac{1}{2\delta\Lambda}\left(\Lambda\left(f(\Omega)+\rho\right) \pm \sqrt{4\delta f(\Omega)\Lambda\mu^A + \Lambda^2\left(f(\Omega)+\rho\right)^2}\right). \tag{29}$$

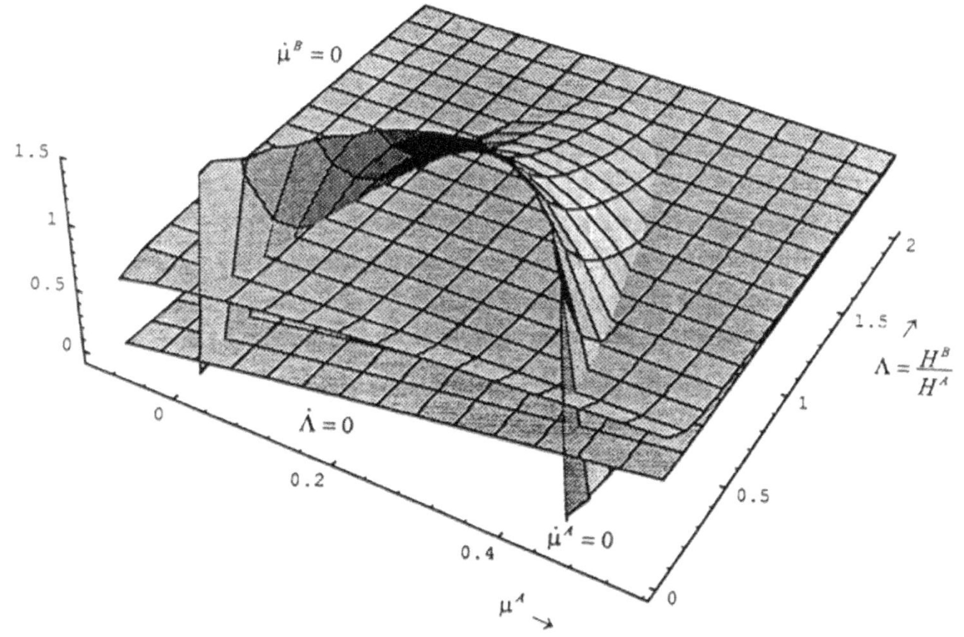

Figure 6.3: A two-country world with technological change

How does this phase diagram change with Ω increasing further? The $\dot{\mu}^B = 0$ plane becomes flatter, until in the limit it is a horizontal line (compare equation (29) $\mu^B \xrightarrow[f(\Omega)\to 0]{} \frac{\rho}{\delta}$). The maximum of the $\dot{\mu}^A = 0$ parabola moves up such that the slopes at the μ^B intercepts become steeper and steeper until, in the limit, the lines are vertical. In order to find initial values chosen by consumers in country j, we subdivide figure 6.3 in two parts, one for Λ greater and one for Λ smaller than 2.

10 This graph was drawn by using Mathematica (cf. Wolfram, 1991).

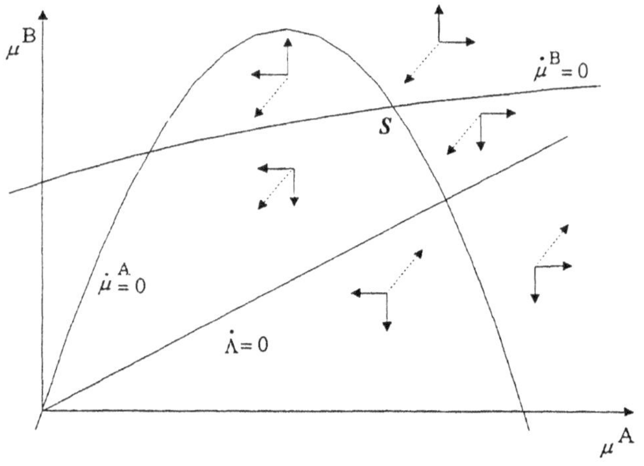

Figure 6.4: The decision problem with technological change

Figure 6.4 represents the first part of figure 6.3 and shows the zero-motion lines for control variables μ^j and state variable Λ in the (μ^A, μ^B) plane, for $\Lambda < 2$. Again, solid lines indicate the direction of motion of control variables and dotted lines of Λ. The same relations hold with respect to zero-motion loci, as in the three-dimensional graph: An increasing Ω will increase the slope of the $\dot{\mu}^A = 0$ and flatten the $\dot{\mu}^B = 0$ line, which, in the limit, gives a phase diagram identical to figure 6.1. Note, however, that here the equilibrium point can never be reached since there will always be an increase of the technological gap. Which are the initial conditions the consumers of country *A* and *B* will choose? By analogy to the phase diagram with no technological progress, we take the intersection point of the $\dot{\mu}^A = 0$ and $\dot{\mu}^B = 0$ line, denoted by *S*, as a candidate for a solution. In this point all equations of motion are satisfied, thus the optimality conditions for both countries are fulfilled. Further, this point approaches the long-run equilibrium point which lies on the $\dot{\Lambda} = 0$ line. An analogue argument to the decision problem with no technological change excludes initial values other than point *S*: Eventually one of the boundaries for μ^j would be reached and one optimality condition would be violated. Since the point S lies within the area $0 < \mu^A, \mu^B < 1$, the optimal initial values constitute an interior solution.

A similar argument can be invoked for the area $\Lambda > 2$. In this case, the $\dot{\mu}^i = 0$ lines do not intersect. The initial conditions for μ^A and μ^B are then chosen such that they will reach the intersection point of the $\dot{\mu}^j = 0$ lines with Λ growing large and $f(\Omega)$ approaching zero. Thus, independently of initial conditions of state variables Λ and Ω, the preceding analysis has shown that the system has well-defined equilibrium trajectories. For the subsequent analysis, it should be retained that an increasing Ω implies that μ^B is always greater than μ^A.

4. Endogenously changing trade patterns

As a benchmark case, consider two economies with no technological change. Then the decision problem of consumers consists in choosing the optimal repartition of human capital between production and education. The last section (cf. figure 6.1) has shown that this leads to an immediate jump on a balanced growth path where both countries allocate the share $\mu^j = \rho/\delta$ to the production sector. Human capital is then accumulated in both countries at the same rate $\delta - \rho$ and the countries' relative factor richness does not change over time[11]. Clearly, in such a situation, initial trade patterns will be observed ever after. If, on the other hand, human capital accumulation does not occur and the evolution of the economies is characterized by technological change only, then the technologically leading country will continuously expand its technological leadership. In our case of no international borrowing or lending, interest rates would not be equalized and the share of the technologically leading country in world expenditure would approach unity.

Let us now turn to the interaction of accumulation of human capital and technological change. In the absence of government intervention and given fixed preferences, the evolution of technology is completely determined by variables out of the range of consumers' influence. Once a country is technologically leading, it will forever expand its leadership. Its innovation rate will approach its autarky innovation rate from below, whereas the other country's innovation rate will become zero in finite time (compare equation (24) and (25)). The accumulation of human capital, however, is determined by an intentional choice of the consumers: If a country is technologically backward (again, say, country A), it will allocate a

[11] Of course, in order that growth rates are positive we need $\rho < \delta$. If this holds then $\mu^j < 1$.

lower share of human capital to production ($\mu^A < \mu^B$) and thus experience a higher human capital accumulation rate, as was shown in the last section. Intuitively, this becomes clear from looking at its budget constraint, which can be expressed by (cf. appendix)

$$\overline{E}^A = c_L \frac{1}{1+\Omega^{(1-\theta)/\theta} L^B/L^A} + (1-c_L)\frac{1}{1+\Lambda \mu^B/\mu^A}.$$

Total expenditure of country A is given by the constant amount $\overline{E}^A$. It can neither increase nor decrease over time, since otherwise the optimality condition (5) would be violated. Since the ratio of intermediate goods Ω increases, the first part of the budget constraint falls and, consequently, its second term must increase which can be achieved only by decreasing the human capital ratio $\Lambda = H^B/H^A$. Thus the technologically backward country A increases human capital more rapidly than country B and vice versa: The country which is technologically leading accumulates human capital at a lower rate than the other country.

Under which circumstances can a change of trade patterns take place? Our assumption that both countries remain incompletely specialized when they open up to trade amounts to requiring that the countries' factor endowments are (and remain) not too dissimilar, a condition which is familiar from static Heckscher-Ohlin models. Since preferences do not differ between countries, an export of the human capital intensive good X by, say, country A is equivalent to an higher output ratio X/Z of that country which, in turn, depends exclusively on factor endowments. In fact, it can be shown that (cf. appendix)

$$\frac{X^A}{Z^A} > \frac{X^B}{Z^B} \Leftrightarrow \frac{\mu^A H^A}{\left(n^A\right)^{\frac{1-\theta}{\theta}} L^A} > \frac{\mu^B H^B}{\left(n^B\right)^{\frac{1-\theta}{\theta}} L^B} \Leftrightarrow \frac{L^B}{L^A}\Omega^{\frac{1-\theta}{\theta}} > \frac{\mu^B}{\mu^A}\Lambda.$$

Thus trade patterns change only if the relative endowment of the economies changes. In our context, where country B is technologically more advanced and its innovation rate is higher than the innovation rate of country A, country A accumulates human capital faster than country B. As a consequence, the dynamic equilibrium is characterized by an increasing Ω and a decreasing Λ. Thus, if the initial conditions are such that country B is human capital richer than country A, then country B will initially export the human capital intensive good. After some time, however, it will be technologically advanced and its endowment with human

capital has fallen relatively to the human capital stock of the other country. These changes may be so large that it then exports the technology intensive good and a change of trade patterns has occurred.
A change of relative factor richness can also occur if human capital accumulation does not take place. An argument for a reversal of trade patterns can then be invoked following the same lines as above. Contrarily, however, interest rates would not be equalized and the technologically leading country would expand its share in world expenditure.

5. Government intervention

The last section has shown that changing trade patterns can occur in this model only if a technologically leading country initially has a relatively low stock of human capital. Such an evolution, however, does not describe the experience of, e.g., Japan in a satisfactory manner since it would imply that all countries which experienced a fundamental change of their economic structure during the last decades were, when beginning to trade with industrialized countries, already technologically leading. Therefore, in this section we turn to government interventions and study how they can influence the evolution of an economy. It should be stressed, that this is a purely positive attempt to re-draw observations and the question, whether these interventions are to be favoured from a welfare point of view, is not a matter of concern here, although it is at least of equal importance and should be at the core of future investigations.
Two natural possibilities come into mind, how a government could intervene: Either research activities are subsidized or the accumulation of human capital is encouraged. We discuss both of these possibilities separately.

R&D subsidies

Many factors influence research and development in an economy; consequently, the government can choose among many possibilities, how to encourage research activities. In the following we will discuss the influence of subsidies to R&D (as e.g. Grossman and Helpman, 1991a, ch. 8).

Costs to produce one new variety are given by $c_R = \phi/n^j$. Let the government commit itself to subsidize each production of a new variety by paying a share s^j of total development costs. Given an innovation rate of ι^j the government's expenditure at every moment is given by $G^j = s^j \phi \iota^j$. These expenditures are financed by lump-sum taxes T^j which changes the aggregate budget constraint of country *j* to[12]

$$E^j + \dot{A}^j = r^j A^j + \phi \iota^j + w_L^j L^j + w_H^j \mu^j H^j - T^j. \tag{30}$$

Due to this subsidy, R&D costs on the *firm* level diminish to $c_R = \phi(1-s^j)/n^j$ and the free-entry condition becomes $\phi(1-s^j)/n^j = v^j(t)$. This modification leaves marginal productivities of factors unchanged and therefore allocation decisions of firms are not influenced, factor price equalization in w_K and w_H still holds (given incomplete specialization) and the same rearrangements and conclusions as in the model without intervention can be undertaken. What changes, however, is the evolution of the technological gap between countries. After modifying equation (23) to include R&D subsidies, the condition whether country *B* increases its technological advance over country *A* does not only depend on current technological differences (represented by the ratio Ω of differentiated goods in country *B* and *A*) but also on R&D subsidies and reads (cf. appendix)

$$\dot{\Omega} \geq 0 \Leftrightarrow \frac{\Omega^{\frac{1-\theta}{\theta}} L^B}{1-s^B} \geq \frac{L^A}{1-s^A}.$$

Let us continue our analysis with the assumption of country *B* being more technologically advanced. If both countries renounce from subsidizing R&D then the technological lead over country *A* would ever increase, thus country *A* might want to intervene[13]. Consider the limiting case that country *A* simply wants to avert falling further behind. Then it chooses (let country *B* be passive, $s^B = 0$) s^A such that

$$s^A = 1 - \frac{L^A}{\Omega^{\frac{1-\theta}{\theta}} L^B}. \tag{31}$$

---

[12] The income effects of R&D subsidies and its effects on the budget constraint are discussed in the appendix. They do not concern the main argument, however.

[13] As mentioned before, the scope of the model is *not* to study normative issues. In this case we would run into difficulties since both countries could subsidize R&D to increase growth rates to infinity, due to the specification of the R&D process.

From this equation interesting implications can be derived. Assume a certain technological lead of country *B*, which translates into a certain $\Omega = \overline{\Omega} > 1$, assuming $L^A = L^B$ for simplicity. Then the share of R&D costs to be paid by country *A* are unambiguously determined by (31). This share, however, might be too high when opening up to trade and approaches unity if the technological gap increases. Thus, in this model it seems advisable, if the technological level is a matter of concern, not to intervene too late.

What happens if s^A is chosen above the critical level which keeps the technological difference at a constant level? Then Ω begins to fall and the technological gap narrows. Thus s^A can be reduced over time to vanish where $n^{B\frac{1-\theta}{\theta}} L^B = n^{A\frac{1-\theta}{\theta}} L^A$.

Combining these results with the analysis undertaken in the last section, it is clear, that these interventions can result in changing trade patterns: Assume that country *A* is technologically backward for some time. It will then certainly be relatively more human capital rich than country *A*. If it subsidizes R&D to such an extent that it becomes the technologically leading country, it will accumulate human capital at a lower rate than country *B*. Provided that this technological lead is extended over time, trade patterns will change from exporting the human capital intensive good *X* to exporting the high-tech good *Z*.

Subsidies to human capital accumulation

Again, one can imagine different ways, how the government could try to foster the accumulation of human capital. A natural suggestion could be to subsidize factor rewards for human capital. One could think that higher rewards for human capital should lead to an increasing share of human capital allocated to the education sector. The individuals' optimizing problem, however, leads to the same optimal behaviour as with no factor reward subsidies. Thus, the aggregate behaviour of the economy does not change and such a policy would fail.

An intervention which does influence human capital accumulation rates, the one we will investigate here, consists in changing the productivity of the education sector which is represented by the parameter δ in human capital accumulation constraint (8). The basic assumption in the following is that this productivity can be increased by investment of the government into the education sector. We will undertake a formal analysis for a two-country world with human capital accumulation *and* technological change. Section 6 will then discuss what happens if technological progress is neglected.

Productivity of the education sector is expressed by $\delta(1+d^j)$, given that the government decides to support the education sector by subsidies d^j. The human capital accumulation constraint (8) then becomes

$$\dot{H}^j = H^j \delta(1+d^j)(1-\mu^j),$$

and the optimality condition concerning the allocation of human capital to the production sector (6) changes to

$$\frac{\dot{w}_H^j}{w_H^j} = r^j - \delta(1+d^j). \tag{32}$$

Factor rewards can still be explicitly computed and we obtain factor price equalization in w_K and w_H. Now, however, factor price equalization does *not* imply interest rate equalization, since education subsidies might differ between countries. Consequently, in contrast to (21), the innovation rate now depends on country *j*'s interest rate r^j

$$\iota^j = (1-\theta)\frac{(n^j)^{\frac{1-\theta}{\theta}} L^j}{(n^A)^{\frac{1-\theta}{\theta}} L^A + (n^B)^{\frac{1-\theta}{\theta}} L^B}\frac{c_L}{\phi} - r^j. \tag{33}$$

What is further needed to discuss the evolution of the two-country world is a relation between interest rates which can be derived from equation (32): By noting that due to incomplete specialization factor prices still equalize and therefore $w_H^A = w_H^B$, this relation can be obtained as

$$r^A = r^B + \delta(1+d^A) - \delta(1+d^B) = r^B + \delta(d^A - d^B),$$

and the budget constraint of one country which can be obtained by following the same steps as in the last section. One finds for country *A*

$$E^A = c_L \frac{L^A}{L^A + \Omega^{\frac{1-\theta}{\theta}} L^B} + (1-c_L)\frac{\mu^A}{\mu^A + \mu^B \Lambda}.$$

Further take into consideration the ratio of human capital endowments and the technological advancement variable Ω. Their timepaths are determined by

$$\dot{\Lambda}/\Lambda = \delta(d^B(1-\mu^B) - d^A(1-\mu^A) + \mu^A - \mu^B),$$

$$\frac{\dot{\Omega}}{\Omega}=(1-\theta)\frac{c_L}{\phi}E\left(\frac{\Omega^{\frac{1-\theta}{\theta}}L^B-L^A}{L^A+\Omega^{\frac{1-\theta}{\theta}}L^B}+\delta\left(d^A-d^B\right)\right).$$

Finally, again, we choose total expenditure as numeraire. Now, however, since interest rates are not equalized (provided that education efforts differ: $d^A \neq d^B$), this choice does not imply that expenditure of each country is constant. We now have

$$E^B=1-E^A, \qquad \dot{E}^A/E^A=r^A-\rho, \qquad \dot{E}^B/E^B=r^A-\delta\left(d^A-d^B\right)-\rho.$$

It can easily be seen that the system behaves just as the two-country world where governments are absent, if both governments undertake the same steps to increase the productivity of their education sector $\left(d^A=d^B\right)$. Now assume that the technologically backward country A undertakes a higher education effort than country B. Then its interest rate is higher $r^A>r^B$ which implies that its share in world expenditure increases. Higher interest rates, however, have a dampening effect on the innovation rate since future profits are discounted at a higher rate, which reduces the present value of a firm. Consequently, R&D costs must not be as high as with lower interest rates and innovation, by (33), is dampened. As a consequence the widening of the technological gap to the other country is speeded up.

On the other hand, if the technologically leading country undertakes education productivity enhancing activities, it can grasp an ever increasing share of world expenditure and at the same time does not loose its technological lead. The effects on trade patterns are obvious: If an increase of the productivity in the education sector leads to a change of the technological leadership, eventually, also trade patterns will change.

6. Conclusion and do countries catch up?

The last sections have shown that there are several mechanisms which can lead to a change of trade patterns. Figure 6.5 summarizes and completes these findings. A distinction is drawn between laissez-faire situations in the first column and government intervention in the second; the different variants of the model are in rows one to three. In a free trade situation, i.e. absence of government intervention, trade patterns reverse if the technologically leading country is initially relatively human capital rich but, after some time, its extending technological leadership overcompensates for human capital abundance. This is represented in the figure by "Initial conditions" and was discussed at the end of section 4. Such a situation can occur both in a world with technological change alone and in a world where technological change and human capital accumulation interact. No change of trade patterns are observed if we allow for human capital accumulation only. It was then argued that the situations of reversal provided by the model did not account in a satisfactory manner for the experience of e.g. Japan. For this reason, government intervention was taken into consideration. We have seen in section 5, that both R&D subsidies, as well as investment into education can lead to trade pattern reversals in a world with both technological change and factor accumulation. This is primarily due to the effect government intervention has on technological leadership. If a government succeeds in increasing the general technological level of the economy sufficiently enough, the country will eventually become an exporter of the high-tech good. These findings can be extended to a simpler world with either technological change or, with an analogous reasoning about the productivity of the education sector, human capital accumulation.

What remains to be discussed is the influence of trade and government intervention on convergence or divergence of expenditure per capita. In figure 6.5, the possibility of catching up or forging ahead, terms taken from Abramovitz (1986), is indicated by an upwards pointing arrow ↗. Catching up/ forging ahead is understood in this context as an increase of a country's share in total world expenditure. Analogously, falling behind is indicated by an downwards pointing arrow ↘. The third arrow is then self-explaining.

Starting again with the free trade situation, one observes that the process of human capital accumulation excludes both catching up as well as falling behind. This is caused by the effect of interest rate equalization: Given that both countries produce both final goods, factor rewards (productivity adjusted for labour) equalize which implies an equalization of the rate of interest as long as both countries accumulate human capital. In terms of accumulation this means that a country compensates its technological backwardness by a higher rate of human capital accumulation exactly to such an extent that its share in world expenditure remains constant.

	Free trade	Government intervention on	
		R&D	Human capital accumulation
Human capital accumulation	No (Section 4)		Yes
	→		↗
Technological change	Initial conditions (Section 4)	Yes	
	↘ (Section 4)	↗	
Technological change and human capital accumulation	Initial conditions (Section 4)	Yes (Section 5)	Yes (Section 5)
	→	→	↗ (Section 5)

Trade pattern reversal
↗ Catching up or forging ahead
↘ Falling behind

Figure 6.5: Trade pattern reversal, catching up and falling behind

In a world characterized by technological change alone, however, strong hysteresis effects can be observed. As mentioned in section 4, a technologically leading country will preserve and extend forever its technological lead and will gain an ever increasing share of world expenditure. In such a situation government subsidies to the R&D process can stop this forging ahead and can induce a catching up process of the technologically backward country. If we allow for human capital accumulation in addition to technological change, however, the above argument on interest rate equalization excludes a catching-up process by means of R&D subsidies: Changes in relative technological levels are compensated by the pace of human capital accumulation. Turning to investment into the education sector, section 5 has analyzed a country in a world where besides human capital accumulation technological change takes place. It was shown that a higher education productivity implies a higher accumulation rate which increases the country's share in total world expenditure. Depending on which country invests more into education, a catching up or a forging ahead process can start. The latter would occur if the technologically leading country also achieves a higher human capital accumulation rate, which would then exclude a compensation for the technological backwardness by the poor country. Analogous findings about investment into the education sector and human capital accumulation rates can be shown to be true if technological change is neglected.

Appendix

1. Individual maximization problem: Deriving equation (5) and (6)

Here we derive the optimal behaviour of consumer i in country j. Her maximization problem with static optimality conditions (2) inserted into the utility function (1), reads

$$\max_{E^i(t),\mu^i(t)} \int_t^\infty \exp[-\rho(\tau-t)]\left(-\ln[P(\tau)]+\ln[E^i(\tau)]\right)d\tau,$$

subject to the budget constraint (3) and the human capital accumulation constraint (4). $P(t)$ is a price index of the form $(p_X/\sigma)^\sigma(p_Z/(1-\sigma))^{(1-\sigma)}$, resulting from static utility maximization. The current-value Hamiltonian associated with this maximization problem is given by

$$\mathcal{H}=-\ln(P)+\ln(E^i)+\eta_{A^i}(r^jA^i+\phi t^i+w_L^j+w_H^j\mu^iH^i-E^i)+\eta_{H^i}H^i\delta(1-\mu^i)$$

The first order conditions are

$$\mathcal{H}_{E^i}=\frac{1}{E^i}-\eta_{A^i}=0\Leftrightarrow\frac{1}{E^i}=\eta_{A^i}, \tag{A.1}$$

$$\mathcal{H}_{\mu^i}=\eta_{A^i}w_H^jH^i-\eta_{H^i}H^i\delta=0\Leftrightarrow\eta_{A^i}w_H^j=\eta_{H^i}\delta, \tag{A.2}$$

and the evolution of costate variables is given by

$$\dot\eta_{A^i}=\rho\eta_{A^i}-\eta_{A^i}r, \tag{A.3}$$

$$\dot{\eta}_{H^i} = \rho\eta_{H^i} - \eta_{A^i} w_H^j \mu^i - \eta_{H^i}\delta(1-\mu^i). \tag{A.4}$$

Substituting controls out of the Hamiltonian with their maximizing values by inserting (A.1) and (A.2), it reads (a similar proceeding is chosen by Benhabib and Perli, 1993)

$$\begin{aligned}\mathcal{H} + \ln(P) &= \ln(E^i) + \eta_{A^i}\left(r^j A^i + \phi\iota^i + w_L^j + w_H^j \mu^i H^i - E^i\right) + \eta_{H^i} H^i \delta(1-\mu^i) \\ &= \ln(E^i) + \eta_{A^i}\left(r^j A^i + \phi\iota^i + w_L^j - E^i\right) + \eta_{A^i} w_H^j \mu^i H^i + \eta_{H^i} H^i \delta - \eta_{H^i}\delta\mu^i H^i \\ &= \ln(E^i) + \eta_{A^i}\left(r^j A^i + \phi\iota^i + w_L^j - E^i\right) + \eta_{H^i} H^i \delta + \left(\eta_{A^i} w_H^j - \eta_{H^i}\delta\right)\mu^i H^i \\ &= \ln(1/\eta_{A^i}) + \eta_{A^i}\left(r^j A^i + \phi\iota^i + w_L^j - E^i\right) + \eta_{H^i} H^i \delta.\end{aligned}$$

Since this modified Hamiltonian is linear in A^i and H^i, it is concave and thus the following transversality conditions are sufficient for optimality.

$$\lim_{\tau\to\infty} \exp[-\rho(\tau-t)]\eta_{A^i}(\tau)A^i(\tau) = 0,$$
$$\lim_{\tau\to\infty} \exp[-\rho(\tau-t)]\eta_{H^i}(\tau)H^i(\tau) = 0.$$

The above optimality conditions can be simplified. Inserting (A.1) into (A.3) gives

$$\frac{\dot{E}^i}{E^i} = r^j - \rho.$$

Equation (A.2) inserted into (A.4) gives $\dot{\eta}_{H^i} / \eta_{H^i} = \rho - \delta$. From equation (A.1) and (A.2) we know $\eta_{H^i} = w_H^j / (\delta E^i)$. Thus

$$\frac{\dot{w}_H}{w_H} - \frac{\dot{E}^i}{E^i} = \rho - \delta. \tag{A.5}$$

Aggregating where an aggregate variable Q follows from individual values Q^i by $Q = \sum_{i=1}^{L^j} Q^i$ gives the equations in the main text.

2. The two-country world: Deriving equations (19) - (23)

The model is given by

$$\frac{\dot{E}^j}{E^j} = r^j - \rho,$$
$$\frac{\dot{w}_H^j}{w_H^j} = r^j - \delta, \tag{A.6}$$
$$E^j + \dot{A}^j = r^j A^j + w_L^j L^j + w_H^j \mu^j H^j + \phi\iota^j,$$
$$\dot{H}^j = H^j \delta(1-\mu^j),$$

$$\frac{\phi}{n^j} = v^j(t) = \int_t^{\infty} \exp\left[-\left(R^j(\tau) - R^j(t)\right)\right]\pi^j(\tau)d\tau, \tag{A.7}$$

$$\pi^j(\tau) = (1-\theta)p_y^j(\tau)y^j(\tau) = (1-\theta)\frac{w_L^j(\tau)}{\theta}\frac{L^j}{n^j(\tau)},$$

$$X^A + X^B = \frac{\sigma}{p_X}\left(E^A + E^B\right),$$

$$Z^A + Z^B = \frac{1-\sigma}{p_Z}\left(E^A + E^B\right),$$

$$p_Z = \left(w_H^j\right)^{\alpha}\left(w_K^j\right)^{1-\alpha},$$

$$p_X = \left(w_H^j\right)^{\beta}\left(w_K^j\right)^{1-\beta},$$

$$a_{KX}\left(w_H^j, w_K^j\right)X^j + a_{KZ}\left(w_H^j, w_K^j\right)Z^j = L^j\left(n^j\right)^{\frac{1-\theta}{\theta}},$$

$$a_{HX}\left(w_H^j, w_K^j\right)X^j + a_{HZ}\left(w_H^j, w_K^j\right)Z^j = \mu^j H^j.$$

Now insert pricing equations into the demand functions and $w_L^j = \theta\left(n^j\right)^{(1-\theta)/\theta} w_K$ into the budget constraint. Note, that country indices can be dropped for human capital wages w_H and the price index w_K, since factor prices are equalized, as long as both countries are incompletely specialized (as we will assume in the following). Further differentiate (A.7) with respect to time to obtain $\iota^j = \dot{n}^j/n^j = \left(\pi^j/v^j\right) - r^j = \left(n^j\pi^j/\phi\right) - r^j$ and insert unit demand functions. Finally, replace $a_{kl}\left(w_H, w_L\right)$ by explicit expressions derived from unit cost functions given in the pricing equations by $\partial c_{kl}\left(w_H, w_L\right)/\partial w_k$. This gives

$$\frac{\dot{E}^j}{E^j} = r^j - \rho, \tag{A.8}$$

$$\frac{\dot{w}_H}{w_H} = r^j - \delta,$$

$$E^j + \dot{A}^j = r^j A^j + \theta\left(n^j\right)^{(1-\theta)/\theta} w_K L^j + w_H \mu^j H^j + \phi\,\iota^j,$$

$$\dot{H}^j = H^j\delta\left(1-\mu^j\right), \tag{A.9}$$

$$\iota^j = \frac{1-\theta}{\theta}w_L^j\frac{L^j}{\phi} - r^j = (1-\theta)\left(n^j\right)^{\frac{1-\theta}{\theta}} w_K\frac{L^j}{\phi} - r^j,$$

$$X^A + X^B = \frac{\sigma}{\left(w_H\right)^{\beta}\left(w_K\right)^{1-\beta}}\left(E^A + E^B\right),$$

$$Z^A + Z^B = \frac{1-\sigma}{\left(w_H\right)^{\alpha}\left(w_K\right)^{1-\alpha}}\left(E^A + E^B\right),$$

$$(1-\beta)\left(\frac{w_H}{w_K}\right)^{\beta} X^j + (1-\alpha)\left(\frac{w_H}{w_K}\right)^{\alpha} Z^j = L^j n^{j\frac{1-\theta}{\theta}},$$

$$\beta\left(\frac{w_K}{w_H}\right)^{1-\beta} X^j + \alpha\left(\frac{w_K}{w_H}\right)^{1-\alpha} Z^j = \mu^j H^j.$$

The equations determining an equilibrium on goods and factor markets (which form a well-known static 2 country 2 good 2 factor equilibrium) can be explicitly solved for factor rewards. First solve factor market clearing conditions for output. This gives (assuming positive values)

$$X^j = \frac{L^j\left(n^j\right)^{\frac{1-\theta}{\theta}}\alpha - \mu^j H^j(1-\alpha)(w_H/w_K)}{(\alpha-\beta)(w_H/w_K)^{\beta}},$$

$$Z^j = \frac{(1-\beta)(w_H/w_K)\mu^j H^j - \beta L^j\left(n^j\right)^{\frac{1-\theta}{\theta}}}{(\alpha-\beta)(w_H/w_K)^{\alpha}}.$$

Inserting these results into goods markets clearing conditions yields after some rearrangement

$$w_K = \frac{c_L}{\left(n^A\right)^{\frac{1-\theta}{\theta}} L^A + \left(n^B\right)^{\frac{1-\theta}{\theta}} L^B} E,\ w_H = \frac{1-c_L}{\mu^A H^A + \mu^B H^B} E. \tag{A.10}$$

where $E = E^A + E^B$ and $c_L = (1-\sigma)(1-\alpha) + \sigma(1-\beta)$, $0 < c_L < 1$. Factor price equalization implies, due to the optimality condition of human capital accumulation, that interest rates equalize. Thus the innovation rate can be written as

$$\iota^j = (1-\theta)\frac{\left(n^j\right)^{\frac{1-\theta}{\theta}} L^j}{\left(n^A\right)^{\frac{1-\theta}{\theta}} L^A + \left(n^B\right)^{\frac{1-\theta}{\theta}} L^B}\frac{c_L E}{\phi} - r. \tag{A.11}$$

We can further write with (A.10)

$$\frac{\dot{w}_H}{w_H} = -\frac{\dot{\mu}^A H^A + \mu^A \dot{H}^A + \dot{\mu}^B H^B + \mu^B \dot{H}^B}{\mu^A H^A + \mu^B H^B} + \frac{\dot{E}}{E} =$$

$$= -\frac{\dot{\mu}^A H^A + \mu^A H^A \delta\left(1-\mu^A\right) + \dot{\mu}^B H^B + \mu^B H^B \delta\left(1-\mu^B\right)}{\mu^A H^A + \mu^B H^B} + \frac{\dot{E}}{E}. \tag{A.12}$$

With $\dot{w}_H/w_H = r - \delta$ and $\dot{E}/E = r - \rho$ this is equivalent to

$$(\delta-\rho)\left(\mu^A H^A + \mu^B H^B\right) = \dot{\mu}^A H^A + \delta\left(\mu^A H^A + \mu^B H^B\right) - \mu^{A^2} H^A \delta + \dot{\mu}^B H^B - \mu^{B^2} H^B \delta \Leftrightarrow$$

$$\mu^A H^A\left(\mu^A \delta - \rho\right) + \mu^B H^B\left(\mu^B \delta - \rho\right) = \dot{\mu}^A H^A + \dot{\mu}^B H^B. \tag{A.13}$$

The budget constraint reads, with $A^j = n^j v^j = \phi$ and the no-arbitrage condition for the asset market written as $r\,A^j = \pi^j n^j - \phi\,\iota^j$,

$$E^j = \pi^j n^j + \theta \frac{{n^j}^{(1-\theta)/\theta}}{\left(n^A\right)^{\frac{1-\theta}{\theta}} L^A + \left(n^B\right)^{\frac{1-\theta}{\theta}} L^B} E\, c_L\, L^j + \frac{1-c_L}{\mu^A H^A + \mu^B H^B} E \mu^j\, H^j .$$

Further, with profits given by

$$\pi^j = (1-\theta)\frac{w_L^j}{\theta}\frac{L^j}{n^j} = (1-\theta){n^j}^{(1-2\theta)/\theta} w_K L^j = (1-\theta)\frac{{n^j}^{(1-2\theta)/\theta}}{\left(n^A\right)^{\frac{1-\theta}{\theta}} L^A + \left(n^B\right)^{\frac{1-\theta}{\theta}} L^B} E c_L\, L^j ,$$

(A.14)

it reads

$$\frac{E^j}{E} = \frac{{n^j}^{(1-\theta)/\theta}}{\left(n^A\right)^{\frac{1-\theta}{\theta}} L^A + \left(n^B\right)^{\frac{1-\theta}{\theta}} L^B} c_L\, L^j + \frac{1-c_L}{\mu^A H^A + \mu^B H^B} \mu^j\, H^j . \tag{A.15}$$

Equations (A.8), (A.9), (A.13), (A.11) and (A.15) (9 equations) determine the time path of E^A, E^B, H^A, H^B, $\mu^A, \mu^B, n^A, n^B, r$.

Since for further analysis only the ratio or the number of middle goods matters, we deduce from the innovation rate equation the time path of $\Omega := n^B / n^A$. It is given by

$$\dot{\Omega} = \left(\iota^B - \iota^A\right)\Omega = (1-\theta)\frac{c_L}{\phi} E \left(\frac{\left(n^B\right)^{\frac{1-\theta}{\theta}} L^B}{\left(n^A\right)^{\frac{1-\theta}{\theta}} L^A + \left(n^B\right)^{\frac{1-\theta}{\theta}} L^B} - \frac{\left(n^A\right)^{\frac{1-\theta}{\theta}} L^A}{\left(n^A\right)^{\frac{1-\theta}{\theta}} L^A + \left(n^B\right)^{\frac{1-\theta}{\theta}} L^B} \right) \Omega$$

$$= (1-\theta)\frac{c_L}{\phi} E \frac{\Omega^{\frac{1-\theta}{\theta}} L^B - L^A}{L^A + \Omega^{\frac{1-\theta}{\theta}} L^B} \Omega .$$

Adding up the aggregate budget constraints of both countries gives

$$\frac{E^A}{E} + \frac{E^B}{E} = \frac{c_L}{\left(n^A\right)^{\frac{1-\theta}{\theta}} L^A + \left(n^B\right)^{\frac{1-\theta}{\theta}} L^B} \left(\left(n^A\right)^{(1-\theta)/\theta} L^A + \left(n^B\right)^{(1-\theta)/\theta} L^B \right)$$

$$+ \frac{1-c_L}{\mu^A H^A + \mu^B H^B} \left(\mu^A\, H^A + \mu^B\, H^B\right) = 1 .$$

Of course, this is Walras' Law. This means that we can drop one budget constraint and choose a numeraire. With total expenditure set equal to unity the interest rate is given by the time preference rate since

$$0 = \frac{\dot{E}}{E} = \frac{\dot{E}^A + \dot{E}^B}{E} = \frac{\dot{E}^A}{E^A}\frac{E^A}{E} + \frac{\dot{E}^B}{E^B}\frac{E^B}{E} = (r-\rho)\left(\frac{E^A}{E} + \frac{E^B}{E}\right) \text{ and } \frac{E^A}{E} + \frac{E^B}{E} > 0 .$$

This implies that total expenditure of both countries is constant.

Concluding, the system now reads

$$\mu^A H^A(\mu^A\delta-\rho)+\mu^B H^B(\mu^B\delta-\rho)=\dot{\mu}^A H^A+\dot{\mu}^B H^B,$$

$$\overline{E}^A=\frac{c_L L^A}{L^A+\Omega^{\frac{1-\theta}{\theta}}L^B}+\frac{1-c_L}{\mu^A H^A+\mu^B H^B}\mu^A H^A,$$

$$\dot{H}^j=H^j\delta(1-\mu^j),$$

$$\dot{\Omega}=(1-\theta)\frac{c_L}{\phi}\frac{\Omega^{\frac{1-\theta}{\theta}}L^B-L^A}{L^A+\Omega^{\frac{1-\theta}{\theta}}L^B}\Omega,$$

Now write the budget constraint as $\overline{E}^A=c_L L^A T+(1-c_L)M$ (A.16)

with $T=\dfrac{1}{L^A+\Omega^{\frac{1-\theta}{\theta}}L^B}$, $M=\dfrac{\mu^A}{\mu^A+\mu^B\Lambda}$,

where $\Lambda=H^B/H^A$ and differentiate with respect to time:

$$\frac{\partial}{\partial t}T=\left(-L^B\frac{1-\theta}{\theta}\Omega^{\frac{1-2\theta}{\theta}}\dot{\Omega}\right)\left(L^A+\Omega^{\frac{1-\theta}{\theta}}L^B\right)^{-2}.$$

$$\frac{\partial}{\partial t}M=\frac{\dot{\mu}^A(\mu^A+\mu^B\Lambda)-(\dot{\mu}^A+\dot{\mu}^B\Lambda+\mu^B\dot{\Lambda})\mu^A}{(\mu^A+\mu^B\Lambda)^2}$$

$$=\frac{1}{(\cdot)^2}(\dot{\mu}^A\mu^A+\dot{\mu}^A\mu^B\Lambda-\mu^A\dot{\mu}^A-\mu^A\dot{\mu}^B\Lambda-\mu^A\mu^B\dot{\Lambda})$$

$$=\frac{1}{(\cdot)^2}(\dot{\mu}^A\mu^B\Lambda-\mu^A\dot{\mu}^B\Lambda-\mu^A\mu^B\dot{\Lambda})=\frac{\mu^A\mu^B\Lambda}{(\cdot)^2}\left(\frac{\dot{\mu}^A}{\mu^A}-\frac{\dot{\mu}^B}{\mu^B}-\frac{\dot{\Lambda}}{\Lambda}\right).$$

Since $\dot{\Lambda}/\Lambda=\delta(1-\mu^B)-\delta(1-\mu^A)=\delta(\mu^A-\mu^B)$ the budget constraint, differentiated with respect to time reads

$$0=c_L\frac{-L^A L^B\frac{1-\theta}{\theta}\Omega^{\frac{1-2\theta}{\theta}}\dot{\Omega}}{\left(L^A+\Omega^{\frac{1-\theta}{\theta}}L^B\right)^2}+(1-c_L)\frac{\mu^A\mu^B\Lambda}{(\mu^A+\mu^B\Lambda)^2}\left(\frac{\dot{\mu}^A}{\mu^A}-\frac{\dot{\mu}^B}{\mu^B}-\delta(\mu^A-\mu^B)\right)\Leftrightarrow$$

$$0=\frac{c_L}{(1-c_L)}\frac{-L^A L^B\frac{1-\theta}{\theta}\Omega^{\frac{1-2\theta}{\theta}}\dot{\Omega}}{\left(L^A+\Omega^{\frac{1-\theta}{\theta}}L^B\right)^2}\frac{(\mu^A+\mu^B\Lambda)^2}{\mu^A\mu^B\Lambda}+\left(\frac{\dot{\mu}^A}{\mu^A}-\frac{\dot{\mu}^B}{\mu^B}-\delta(\mu^A-\mu^B)\right).$$

With $$\widehat{O}=\frac{c_L}{(1-c_L)}\frac{-L^A L^B\frac{1-\theta}{\theta}\Omega^{\frac{1-2\theta}{\theta}}\dot{\Omega}}{\left(L^A+\Omega^{\frac{1-\theta}{\theta}}L^B\right)^2}\frac{\left(\mu^A+\mu^B\Lambda\right)^2}{\mu^A\mu^B\Lambda}$$

$$=\frac{-c_L^2}{(1-c_L)}\frac{(1-\theta)^2}{\phi\theta}\frac{L^A L^B\Omega^{\frac{1-\theta}{\theta}}\left(\Omega^{\frac{1-\theta}{\theta}}L^B-L^A\right)}{\left(L^A+\Omega^{\frac{1-\theta}{\theta}}L^B\right)^3}\frac{\left(\mu^A+\mu^B\Lambda\right)^2}{\mu^A\mu^B\Lambda}$$

$$\equiv -f(\Omega)\frac{\left(\mu^A+\mu^B\Lambda\right)^2}{\mu^A\mu^B\Lambda},$$

this can be written as

$$\mu^{A^{-1}}\dot{\mu}^A-\mu^{B^{-1}}\dot{\mu}^B=-\widehat{O}+\delta\mu^A-\delta\mu^B. \tag{A.17}$$

The optimality condition for the allocation of human capital (A.13) can be written as

$$\dot{\mu}^A+\Lambda\dot{\mu}^B=\mu^A\left(\mu^A\delta-\rho\right)+\mu^B\Lambda\left(\mu^B\delta-\rho\right). \tag{A.18}$$

Solving these two equations for $\dot{\mu}^A$ and $\dot{\mu}^B$ with $D=\left(\Lambda/\mu^A\right)+\left(1/\mu^B\right)$ gives

$$\begin{aligned}
\dot{\mu}^A D &=\left(-\widehat{O}+\delta\mu^A-\delta\mu^B\right)\Lambda+\left(\mu^A\left(\mu^A\delta-\rho\right)+\mu^B\Lambda\left(\mu^B\delta-\rho\right)\right)\mu^{B^{-1}}\\
&=-\widehat{O}\Lambda+\delta\mu^A\Lambda-\delta\mu^B\Lambda+\mu^{A^2}\delta/\mu^B-\mu^A\rho/\mu^B+\Lambda\mu^B\delta-\Lambda\rho\\
&=-\widehat{O}\Lambda+\delta\mu^A\Lambda+\mu^{A^2}\delta/\mu^B-\mu^A\rho/\mu^B-\Lambda\rho\\
&=-\widehat{O}\Lambda+\Lambda\left(\mu^A\delta-\rho\right)+\mu^A/\mu^B\left(\mu^A\delta-\rho\right)\\
&=-\widehat{O}\Lambda+\left(\mu^B\Lambda+\mu^A\right)\left(\mu^A\delta-\rho\right)/\mu^B.
\end{aligned}$$

$$\begin{aligned}
\dot{\mu}^B D &=\mu^{A^{-1}}\left(\mu^A\left(\mu^A\delta-\rho\right)+\mu^B\Lambda\left(\mu^B\delta-\rho\right)\right)-\left(-\widehat{O}+\delta\mu^A-\delta\mu^B\right)\\
&=\left(\mu^A\delta-\rho\right)+\mu^B\mu^{A^{-1}}\Lambda\left(\mu^B\delta-\rho\right)+\widehat{O}-\delta\mu^A+\delta\mu^B\\
&=\mu^A\delta-\rho+\mu^{B^2}\mu^{A^{-1}}\Lambda\delta-\mu^B\mu^{A^{-1}}\Lambda\rho+\widehat{O}-\delta\mu^A+\delta\mu^B\\
&=\widehat{O}+\left(\mu^A+\Lambda\mu^B\right)\left(\mu^B\delta-\rho\right)/\mu^A.
\end{aligned}$$

With D and $\widehat{O}$ inserted, this gives

$$\begin{aligned}
\dot{\mu}^A &=\frac{f(\Omega)\frac{\left(\mu^A+\mu^B\Lambda\right)^2}{\mu^A\mu^B\Lambda}}{\Lambda/\mu^A+1/\mu^B}\Lambda+\frac{\left(\mu^B\Lambda+\mu^A\right)\left(\mu^A\delta-\rho\right)}{\left(\Lambda/\mu^A+1/\mu^B\right)\mu^B}\\
&=f(\Omega)\left(\mu^A+\mu^B\Lambda\right)+\mu^A\left(\mu^A\delta-\rho\right).
\end{aligned}$$

$$\dot{\mu}^B = \frac{-f(\Omega)\dfrac{\left(\mu^A+\mu^B\Lambda\right)^2}{\mu^A\mu^B\Lambda}}{\Lambda/\mu^A+1/\mu^B} + \frac{\left(\mu^A+\Lambda\mu^B\right)\left(\mu^B\delta-\rho\right)}{\left(\Lambda/\mu^A+1/\mu^B\right)\mu^A} =$$

$$= -f(\Omega)\left(\mu^A\Lambda^{-1}+\mu^B\right)+\mu^B\left(\mu^B\delta-\rho\right).$$

Thus the reduced form of our two-country world has the relatively neat form

$$\dot{\mu}^A = f(\Omega)\left(\mu^A+\mu^B\Lambda\right)+\mu^A\left(\mu^A\delta-\rho\right),$$

$$\dot{\mu}^B = -f(\Omega)\left(\mu^A\Lambda^{-1}+\mu^B\right)+\mu^B\left(\mu^B\delta-\rho\right),$$

$$\dot{\Lambda} = \delta\left(\mu^A-\mu^B\right)\Lambda,$$

$$\dot{\Omega} = (1-\theta)\frac{c_L}{\phi}\frac{\Omega^{(1-\theta)/\theta}L^A-L^B}{L^A+\Omega^{(1-\theta)/\theta}L^B}\Omega.$$

3. Zero-motion loci in figure 6.3: Deriving equations (26) - (28)

$$\dot{\mu}^A \geq 0 \Leftrightarrow f(\Omega)\left(\mu^A+\mu^B\Lambda\right) \geq -\mu^A\left(\mu^A\delta-\rho\right) \Leftrightarrow$$

$$\Leftrightarrow \mu^B \geq -\frac{\mu^A}{\Lambda}\left(\left(\mu^A\delta-\rho\right)f(\Omega)^{-1}+1\right).$$

$$\dot{\mu}^B \geq 0 \Leftrightarrow f(\Omega)\left(\mu^A\Lambda^{-1}+\mu^B\right) \leq \mu^B\left(\mu^B\delta-\rho\right) \Leftrightarrow$$

$$\Leftrightarrow \mu^A\Lambda^{-1}+\mu^B \leq \mu^B\left(\mu^B\delta-\rho\right)f(\Omega)^{-1} \Leftrightarrow \mu^A \leq \mu^B\Lambda\left(\left(\mu^B\delta-\rho\right)f(\Omega)^{-1}-1\right).$$

The first inequality can be easily plotted (as an equality) for given Λ and μ^A. The second inequality, solved for μ^B gives

$$\mu^B = \frac{1}{2\delta\Lambda}\left(\Lambda\left(f(\Omega)+\rho\right)\pm\sqrt{4\delta f(\Omega)\Lambda\mu^A+\Lambda^2\left(f(\Omega)+\rho\right)^2}\right).$$

4. The extrema of f(Ω)

Find candidates for extrema of

$$f(\Omega) := \frac{c_L^2}{(1-c_L)}\frac{(1-\theta)^2}{\phi\theta}L^A L^B \Omega^{\frac{1-\theta}{\theta}}\left(\Omega^{\frac{1-\theta}{\theta}}L^B-L^A\right)\left(L^A+\Omega^{\frac{1-\theta}{\theta}}L^B\right)^{-3}.$$

To this end, rewrite this function as $f(\Omega)=\kappa\frac{N\left(N-L^{A}\right)}{\left(L^{A}+N\right)^{3}}$ with κ constant and $N=\Omega^{\frac{1-\theta}{\theta}}L^{B}$ and observe that the first order condition for extrema reads $\frac{\partial f(\Omega)}{\partial N}\frac{\partial N}{\partial\Omega}=0$. This is fulfilled if $\frac{\partial f(\Omega)}{\partial N}=0$ since $\frac{\partial N}{\partial\Omega}\neq 0$. Now compute

$$\frac{\partial}{\partial N}\kappa\frac{N\left(N-L^{A}\right)}{\left(L^{A}+N\right)^{3}}=\kappa\frac{\left(2N-L^{A}\right)\left(L^{A}+N\right)^{3}-N\left(N-L^{A}\right)3\left(L^{A}+N\right)^{2}}{\left(L^{A}+N\right)^{6}}=0\Leftrightarrow$$

$$\left(2N-L^{A}\right)\left(L^{A}+N\right)-3N\left(N-L^{A}\right)=0\Leftrightarrow$$

$$2NL^{A}-L^{A^{2}}+2N^{2}-NL^{A}-3N^{2}+3NL^{A}=0\Leftrightarrow N^{2}-4NL^{A}+L^{A^{2}}=0\Leftrightarrow$$

$N_{1,2}=\frac{4L^{A}\pm\sqrt{16L^{A^{2}}-4L^{A^{2}}}}{2}=L^{A}\left(2\pm\sqrt{3}\right)$. Thus we have candidates for extrema at $\Omega_{1,2}=\left(\frac{L^{A}}{L^{B}}\left(2\pm\sqrt{3}\right)\right)^{\frac{\theta}{1-\theta}}$ and $\Omega_{3}=0$. Since $f(\Omega)<0$ for $0<\Omega<\left(L^{A}/L^{B}\right)^{\frac{\theta}{1-\theta}}$ and $f(\Omega)>0$ for $\Omega>\left(L^{A}/L^{B}\right)^{\frac{\theta}{1-\theta}}$, $\Omega_{1}=\left(\frac{L^{A}}{L^{B}}\left(2-\sqrt{3}\right)\right)^{\frac{\theta}{1-\theta}}$ is a minimum and $\Omega_{2}=\left(\frac{L^{A}}{L^{B}}\left(2+\sqrt{3}\right)\right)^{\frac{\theta}{1-\theta}}$ is a maximum.

5. Deriving the consumer's budget constraint, p. 126

cf. equation (A.16)

6. The relation between output ratio and factor endowment, p. 126

We show that $\frac{X^{A}}{Z^{A}}>\frac{X^{B}}{Z^{B}}\Leftrightarrow\frac{\mu^{B}H^{B}}{\left(n^{B}\right)^{\frac{1-\theta}{\theta}}L^{B}}>\frac{\mu^{A}H^{A}}{\left(n^{A}\right)^{\frac{1-\theta}{\theta}}L^{A}}$.

Solving (17) and (18) for output gives

$$X^j = \frac{1}{D^j}\left(L^j\left(n^j\right)^{\frac{(1-\theta)}{\theta}} a_{HZ}\left(w_H^j, w_K^j\right) - \mu^j H^j a_{KZ}\left(w_H^j, w_K^j\right) \right) \text{ and}$$

$$Z^j = \frac{1}{D^j}\left(a_{KX}\left(w_H^j, w_K^j\right)\mu^j H^j - a_{HX}\left(w_H^j, w_K^j\right) L^j\left(n^j\right)^{\frac{1-\theta}{\theta}} \right).$$

Thus $\frac{X^A}{Z^A} > \frac{X^B}{Z^B} \Leftrightarrow$[14] $\frac{L^A\left(n^A\right)^{\frac{1-\theta}{\theta}} a_{HZ} - \mu^A H^A a_{KZ}}{a_{KX}\mu^A H^A - a_{HX} L^A\left(n^A\right)^{\frac{1-\theta}{\theta}}} > \frac{L^B\left(n^B\right)^{\frac{1-\theta}{\theta}} a_{HZ} - \mu^B H^B a_{KZ}}{a_{KX}\mu^B H^B - a_{HX} L^B\left(n^B\right)^{\frac{1-\theta}{\theta}}} \Leftrightarrow$:

$$\frac{\tilde{L}^A a_{HZ} - \tilde{H}^A a_{KZ}}{a_{KX}\tilde{H}^A - a_{HX}\tilde{L}^A} > \frac{\tilde{L}^B a_{HZ} - \tilde{H}^B a_{KZ}}{a_{KX}\tilde{H}^B - a_{HX}\tilde{L}^B},$$

where a tilde indicates the effective quantity of factors in the production process. This is equivalent to (note, that both denominators are negative since $a_{KX}\tilde{H}^j - a_{HX}\tilde{L}^j < 0 \Leftrightarrow \tilde{H}^j/\tilde{L}^j < a_{HX}/a_{KX}$ and $\tilde{H}^j/\tilde{L}^j < a_{HX}/a_{KX}$ because X is the human capital intensive good)

$$a_{KX}\tilde{H}^B\tilde{L}^A a_{HZ} - a_{KX}\tilde{H}^B\tilde{H}^A a_{KZ} - a_{HX}\tilde{L}^B\tilde{L}^A a_{HZ} + a_{HX}\tilde{L}^B\tilde{H}^A a_{KZ} >$$
$$> a_{KX}\tilde{H}^A\tilde{L}^B a_{HZ} - a_{KX}\tilde{H}^A\tilde{H}^B a_{KZ} - a_{HX}\tilde{L}^A\tilde{L}^B a_{HZ} + a_{HX}\tilde{L}^A\tilde{H}^B a_{KZ} \Leftrightarrow$$
$$\left(a_{KX}a_{HZ} - a_{HX}a_{KZ}\right)\tilde{H}^B\tilde{L}^A + \left(a_{HX}a_{KZ} - a_{KX}a_{HZ}\right)\tilde{L}^B\tilde{H}^A > 0.$$

The expression in the first brackets is negative, again because X is the human capital intensive good. Concluding, we find

$$\frac{X^A}{Z^A} > \frac{X^B}{Z^B} \Leftrightarrow -\tilde{H}^B\tilde{L}^A + \tilde{L}^B\tilde{H}^A > 0 \Leftrightarrow \frac{\mu^A H^A}{\left(n^A\right)^{\frac{1-\theta}{\theta}} L^A} > \frac{\mu^B H^B}{\left(n^B\right)^{\frac{1-\theta}{\theta}} L^B}.$$

7. Government intervention

R&D subsidies

With R&D subsidies, the innovation rate of country j becomes

[14] Here we take factor price equalization as given.

$$\iota^j = (1-\theta)\frac{n^{j\frac{1-\theta}{\theta}}L^j}{\left(n^A\right)^{\frac{1-\theta}{\theta}}L^A + \left(n^B\right)^{\frac{1-\theta}{\theta}}L^B}\frac{c_L E}{\phi\left(1-s^j\right)} - r.$$

Computing $\dot{\Omega}$, one obtains

$$\dot{\Omega} = (1-\theta)\frac{c_L}{\phi}E\left(\frac{\left(n^B\right)^{\frac{1-\theta}{\theta}}L^B\left(1-s^B\right)^{-1}}{\left(n^A\right)^{\frac{1-\theta}{\theta}}L^A + \left(n^B\right)^{\frac{1-\theta}{\theta}}L^B} - \frac{\left(n^A\right)^{\frac{1-\theta}{\theta}}L^A\left(1-s^A\right)^{-1}}{\left(n^A\right)^{\frac{1-\theta}{\theta}}L^A + \left(n^B\right)^{\frac{1-\theta}{\theta}}L^B}\right)\Omega$$

$$= (1-\theta)\frac{c_L}{\phi}E\frac{\Omega^{\frac{1-\theta}{\theta}}L^B\left(1-s^B\right)^{-1} - L^A\left(1-s^A\right)^{-1}}{L^A + \Omega^{\frac{1-\theta}{\theta}}L^B}\Omega.$$

Thus the condition for $\dot{\Omega} > 0$ becomes $\frac{\Omega^{\frac{1-\theta}{\theta}}L^B}{1-s^B} > \frac{L^A}{1-s^A}$.

Budget constraint

Now consider the budget constraints. Total wealth still equals $A^j = \phi$ but the equilibrium condition for the asset market now reads $r A^j = \pi^j n^j - \phi\left(1-s^j\right)\iota^j$. Inserting this into the budget constraint it changes to

$$E^j = \pi^j n^j - \phi\left(1-s^j\right)\iota^j + w_L^j L^j + w_H^j \mu^j H^j + \phi\,\iota^j - T^j$$
$$= \pi^j n^j + \phi\,\iota^j s^j + w_L^j L^j + w_H^j \mu^j H^j - T^j.$$

Now insert factor rewards and find (remember that $w_L^j = \theta\left(n^j\right)^{(1-\theta)/\theta} w_K$)

$$E^j = \pi^j n^j + \phi\,\iota^j s^j + \theta\frac{\left(n^j\right)^{(1-\theta)/\theta}}{\left(n^A\right)^{\frac{1-\theta}{\theta}}L^A + \left(n^B\right)^{\frac{1-\theta}{\theta}}L^B}Ec_L L^j + \frac{1-c_L}{\mu^A H^A + \mu^B H^B}E\mu^j H^j - T^j.$$

Profits are still given by (A.14), total taxes are given by $T^j = \phi\,\iota^j s^j$, thus the budget constraint is identical to equation (A.15). This simply means that the taxes to be paid by the consumers in a country are compensated by the increasing income from R&D due to a higher rate of innovation. This implies that, in this model, a government could subsidize R&D costs such that infinite innovation rates result, without any social costs[15]. Clearly, this is due to the simplified specification of the R&D activity. Since the model is not used for normative analysis, however, this does not really present a problem.

[15] I would like to thank Paul Tang, who has pointed out to me the absence of social costs of the R&D process as specified here.

References

Abramovitz, M., 1986, Catching up, forging ahead, and falling behind. Journal of Economic History 46: 385 - 406.

Alogoskoufis, G., van der Ploeg, F., 1991a, On budgetary policies, growth, and external deficits in an interdependent world. Journal of the Japanese and International Economics 4: 305 - 24.

Alogoskoufis, G., van der Ploeg, F., 1991b, Debts, deficits and growth in interdependent economies. CEPR Discussion Paper 533, London.

Araujo, A. , Scheinkman, J. A., 1983, Maximum principle and transversality condition for concave infinite horizon economic models. Journal of Economic Theory 30: 1 - 16.

Arrow, K. J., 1968, Applications of control theory to economic growth. In Dantzig, G. B., Veinott, A. F. Jr. (eds.), Mathematics of the decision sciences, Part 2. American Mathematical Society, Providence.

Arrow, K. J., Kurz, M., 1970, Public investment, the rate of return and optimal fiscal policy. Baltimore, Johns Hopkins University Press.

Balassa, B., Noland, M., 1989, The changing comparative advantage of Japan and the United States. Journal of the Japanese and International Economies 3: 174 - 187.

Barro, R. J., 1974, Are government bonds net wealth? Journal of Political Economy 82: 1095 - 1117.

Barro, R. J., 1990, Government spending in a simple model of endogenous growth. Journal of Political Economy 98: S103 - S125.

Barro, R. J., Sala-i-Martin, X., 1992, Public finance in models of economic growth. Review of Economic Studies 59: 645 - 661.

Benhabib, J., Perli, R., 1993, Uniqueness and indeterminacy: Transitional dynamics in a model of endogenous growth. C. V. Starr Center Research Reports, New York University.

Berck, P., Sydsaeter, K., 1991, Economists' mathematical manual. Berlin, Springer.

Blanchard, O. J., 1985, Debt, deficits, and finite horizon. Journal of Political Economy 93: 223 - 48.

Blanchard, O. J., Fischer, S., 1989, Lectures on macroeconomics. Cambridge, Massachusetts, MIT Press.

Braun, M., 1975, Differential equations and their applications (short version). Berlin, Springer.

Buiter, W. H., 1981, Time preference and international lending and borrowing in an overlapping generations model. Journal of Political Economy 89: 769 - 797.

Buiter, W. H., 1988, Death, birth, productivity growth and debt neutrality. The Economic Journal 98: 279 - 293.

Buiter, W. H., Kletzer, K. M., 1991, Persistent differences in national productivity growth rates with common technology and free capital mobility: The roles of private thrift, public debt, capital taxation and policy towards human capital formation. Journal of the Japanese and International Economics 5: 325 - 53.

Burmeister, E., Dobell, A. R., 1970, Mathematical theories of economic growth. London, Macmillan.

Chiang, A., C., 1974, Fundamental methods of mathematical economics. New York, McGraw-Hill.

Chiang, A., C., 1992, Elements of dynamic optimization. New York, McGraw-Hill.

Devereux, M. B., Lapham, B. J., 1993, The stability of economic integration and endogenous growth. Institute for Economic Research, Discussion Paper 878. University of British Columbia.

Dinopoulos, E., Oehmke, J. F., Segerstrom, P. S., 1993, High-technology-industry trade and investment. Journal of International Economics 34: 49 - 71.

Dixit, A. K., Norman, V., 1980, Theory of international trade. Cambridge, Cambridge University Press.

Dixit, A., K. Stiglitz, 1977, Monopolistic competition and optimum product diversity. American Economic Review 67: 297 - 308.

Ethier, W. J., 1982, National and international returns to scale in the modern theory of international trade. American Economic Review 72: 389 - 405.

Faig, M., 1991, A simple economy with human capital: Transitional dynamics, technology shocks, and fiscal policies. Working Paper no. 9121, University of Toronto.

Feenstra, R., 1990, Trade and uneven growth. NBER Working Paper 3276. Cambridge, Massachusetts.

Feichtinger, G., Hartl, R. F., 1986, Optimale Kontrolle ökonomischer Prozesse. Berlin, DeGruyter.

Gandolfo, G., 1986, International economics. Berlin, Springer.

Grossman, G. M., 1990, Explaining Japan's innovation and growth: A model of quality competition and dynamic comparative advantage. Bank of Japan Monetary and Economic Studies 8: 75 - 100.

Grossman, G. M., Helpman, E., 1989, Product development and international trade. Journal of Political Economy 97: 1261 - 1283.

Grossman, G. M., Helpman, E., 1990, Comparative advantage and long-run growth. American Economic Review 80: 796 - 815.

Grossman, G. M., Helpman, E., 1991a, Innovation and growth in the global economy. Cambridge, Massachusetts, MIT Press.

Grossman, G. M., Helpman, E., 1991b, Quality ladders and product cycle. Quarterly Journal of Economics 106: 557 - 586.

Helpman, E., 1981, International trade in the presence of product differentiation, economies of scale and monopolistic competition. A Chamberlin-Heckscher-Ohlin approach. Journal of International Economics 11: 305 - 340.

Helpman, E., P. Krugman, 1985, Market structure and foreign trade. Cambridge, Massachusetts, MIT Press.

Hirsch, S., 1967, Location of industry and international competitiveness. London, Oxford University Press.

Lawrence, C., P. T. Spiller, 1983, Product diversity, economies of scale, and international trade. Quarterly Journal of Economics 97: 63 - 83.

Léonard, D., Long, N. V., 1992, Optimal control theory and static optimization in economics. Cambridge, Cambridge University Press.

Lorenz, H. W., 1989, Nonlinear dynamical economics and chaotic motion. Berlin, Springer.

Lucas, R. E., 1988, On the mechanics of economic development. Journal of Monetary Economics 22: 3 - 42.

Lucas, R. E., 1993, Making a miracle. Econometrica 61: 251 - 272.

Mangasarian, O. L., 1966, Sufficient conditions for the optimal control of non linear systems. SIAM Journal on Control 4: 139 - 152.

Mulligan, C. B., 1991, A note on the time elimination method for solving recursive dynamic economic models. NBER Technical Working Paper 116, Cambridge, Massachusetts.

Mulligan, C. B., Sala-i-Martin, X., 1993, Transitional dynamics in two-sector models of endogenous growth. Quarterly Journal of Economics 108: 739 - 773.

Rebelo, S., 1988, Essays on growth and business cycles. Ph. D. dissertation, University of Rochester.

Rebelo, S., 1991, Long-Run Policy Analysis and Long-Run Growth. Journal of Political Economy 99: 500 - 521.

Rebelo, S., 1992, Growth in Open Economies. Carnegie-Rochester Conference Series on Public Policy 36: 5 - 46.

Rivera-Batiz, L. A., Romer, P. M., 1991, Economic integration and endogenous growth. The Quarterly Journal of Economics 106: 531 - 555.

Rivera-Batiz, L. A., Xie, D., 1993, Integration among unequals. Regional Science and Urban Economics 23: 337 - 354.

Romer, P. M., 1986, Increasing returns and long-run growth. Journal of Political Economy 94: 1002 - 1037.

Romer, P. M., 1987, Growth based on increasing returns due to specialization. American Economic Review 77: 56 - 62.

Romer, P. M., 1990, Endogenous technological change. Journal of Political Economy 98, S71 - S102.

Sala-i-Martin, X., 1990, Lecture notes on economics growth I: Introduction to the literature and neoclassical models. NBER Working Paper 3563, Cambridge, Massachusetts.

Shimomura, K., 1993, Durable consumption goods and the pattern of international trade. In Herberg, H., Long, N. V. (eds.), Trade, welfare, and economic policies, Essays in honor of Murray C. Kemp. Ann Arbor, The University of Michigan Press.

Solow, R. M., 1956, A contribution to the theory of economic growth. Quarterly Journal of Economics 70: 65 - 94.

Stiglitz, J. E., 1970, Factor price equalization in a dynamic economy. Journal of Political Economy 78: 456 - 488.

Vernon, R., 1966, International investment and international trade in the product cycle. Quarterly Journal of Economics 80: 190 - 207.

Vernon, R., 1987, Product cycles. The New Palgrave, London, Macmillan Press.

Wälde, K., 1994a, On an additional condition for factor-price equalisation in intertemporal Heckscher-Ohlin models. Economics Letters 44: 411 - 414.

Wälde, K., 1994b, Unequal factor rewards and incomplete specialization in a Heckscher-Ohlin model of endogenous growth. Journal of Economics 59: 311 - 323.

Weil, Ph., 1987, Permanent budget deficits and inflation. Journal of Monetary Economics 20: 393 - 410.

Wolfram, 1991, Mathematica, A system for doing mathematics by computer. New York, Addison Wesley.

World Bank, 1993, The East Asian miracle. Economic growth and public policy, A World Bank policy research report, Oxford University Press, Oxford.

GPSR Compliance

The European Union's (EU) General Product Safety Regulation (GPSR) is a set of rules that requires consumer products to be safe and our obligations to ensure this.

If you have any concerns about our products, you can contact us on ProductSafety@springernature.com

In case Publisher is established outside the EU, the EU authorized representative is:

Springer Nature Customer Service Center GmbH
Europaplatz 3
69115 Heidelberg, Germany

Batch number: 10732714

Printed by Printforce, the Netherlands